AURICULAS FOR EVERYONE

AURICULAS FOR EVERYONE

HOW TO GROW AND SHOW PERFECT PLANTS

MARY A. ROBINSON

GUILD OF MASTER CRAFTSMAN
PUBLICATIONS LTD

First published 2000 by
Guild of Master Craftsman Publications Ltd,
166 High Street, Lewes,
East Sussex BN7 1XU

Photographs by Michael and Mary A. Robinson, except for:
Ken Whorton, 'Bacchante', 'Bella' and 'Cameo Beauty' on page 103,
'Crimson Glow' on p 105, 'Fantasia', 'Gold Seal' and 'Golden Hind' on
p 107, 'Grand Slam' on p 108, 'Paphos' on page 111, 'Sarah Gisby' on p 113
and 'Trouble' on page 114 ;
Derek Salt, Double auriculas on p 101, 'Fred Booley' on p 107, 'Gwen
Baker' and 'Lincoln Imp' on p 109
and 'Terror-cotta' on p 113;
William and Simon Lockyer, 'Dales Red' on pp 91 and 93,
'Lavender Lady' on p 94, 'Lockyers Frilly', 'Lockyer's Gem' on p 95
and 'Queen Alexandra' on p 97;
Brenda Hyatt auricula display on p 11
David Bradford, aphids and ants on p 52, devil's coach-horse on p 53,
cabbage white caterpillars on p 54, slug on p 57 and snail on p 58
Bruce Coleman Collection/Dr Frieder Sauer, ground beetle on p 53;
Sir Jeremy Grayson, hoverfly on p 53; Kim Taylor, lacewing on p 53;
National Trust Photographic Library/Stephen Robson,
auricula theatre on p 30
The Northern Section of the National Auricula and
Primula Society, auricula display on p 16, show standard
'Scipio' on p 45, 'Toot Toot Tootsie' on p 47

ISBN 1 86108 149 9
A catalogue record of this book is available from the British Library.

Designed by Joyce Chester
Cover design by Ian Smith, Guild of Master Craftsman Design Studio
Typefaces: Sabon, Frutiger and Lithos

Colour origination by Viscan Graphics (Singapore)
Printed and bound by Kyodo Printing (Singapore) under the supervision of
MRM Graphics, Winslow, Buckinghamshire, UK

ACKNOWLEDGEMENTS

Jack Barker, of Great Bookham, for allowing me to use the
information he is gathering to write a book on
'The House of Douglas'
Brenda Hyatt, for patiently providing information on
numerous auriculas
Derek Salt, for the loan of his slides and providing
information on Doubles
William and Simon Lockyer, for the loan of their slides and
providing information on Borders
Allan Guest for information on fancies and stripes

CONTENTS

TRIBUTE

Mary touched the lives of many people with her friendly,
common-sense approach in all that she did.

Following on from her University days, our marriage and young family kept her busy,
but she became increasingly interested in her auriculas, soon realizing
just how addictive they can be. Although her collection took time and patience, her
dream began to come true when we moved to our nursery at Hemswell,
and over time, Mary's enthusiasm for her plants became well known
throughout this country [England] and beyond.

She will always be remembered for her generosity to new growers,
giving everyone the chance to share the flowers she loved.

It is my dearest wish that this book will be a lasting tribute
to her lifetime's love of auriculas.

Michael Robinson

PUBLISHERS' NOTE

Mary put a lot of time and thought into the presentation and
writing of this book and handed us a beautifully crafted manuscript.
Sadly, she died before its publication.

We are fortunate that she was well-known and respected in her field;
she had many friends who were very generous with their time and advice
in helping us with its production.

INTRODUCTION

EVERY GARDENER can find a suitable area to grow a few of these wonderful plants, be it the vigorous and easy garden hybrids, the Alpines, Borders and Doubles, or the exotic Show auriculas. Auriculas are for everyone.

In general, auriculas are easy to grow, but considerable skill and devotion is needed to achieve top show-quality flowers, either for your own benefit or to stage at the auricula shows. The joy in growing auriculas is not confined to the plants themselves; their history contributes greatly to the fascination inspired by the wonderful range of colours and forms to be found within this group of plants.

The purpose of this book is to introduce the novice grower to the joys and mysteries of the auricula by presenting the basic knowledge necessary for growing auriculas successfully in a straightforward manner.

Too often gardening books become bogged down with botanical terms, and rather than being a pleasure to read they become a frustrating nightmare. This book provides as much information and as many photographs of auriculas as space will allow.

Photographing auriculas is not easy, especially the blues and purples, so please forgive the printers and myself for any colours which do not seem correct. I must stress that most of the photographs are not of plants groomed to show standards, but of plants from our collection.

The gardening press, usually due to the sin of omission, often fails to make it clear that the glorious Show auriculas, with their green and grey **edges**, are not plants for the garden. There are many other lovely auriculas that will prosper in a shady corner, and this book is designed to help the gardener choose the plants suitable for the particular conditions in their own gardens.

We have been growing auriculas at Martin Nest Nurseries for 20 years, initially in the Pennines near Huddersfield, then, since 1986, at Hemswell, near Gainsborough in Lincolnshire (both in the UK). We started growing and collecting them because of the attractions of the plant, and our collection has been built up over many years. We have always sold any surplus, but up to about 1990 the collection was not a commercial enterprise – it was then we realized that, in order to look after and increase our collection, it was necessary for it to be economically viable. Not every variety had to pay its own way, but the collection as a whole had to. We grow many auriculas that **offset** so slowly they will never be a commercial proposition, but we feel that preserving these varieties is of importance to the future of the auricula.

Our closest ties are with the Northern Section of the National Auricula and Primula Society, but we also have many friends and acquaintances in the Midland and West, and Southern Sections. In fact, it was the well-known southern grower, Brenda Hyatt, a friend for many years, who encouraged us to apply for National Collection status, as she felt that our collection was worthy. In 1996 we were awarded this status, which inevitably led to the collecting and documenting of even more data regarding the auriculas we grow. As with any form of gardening, the biggest lesson you learn is how little you really know.

The auricula is now achieving worldwide recognition. There are nurseries in America, Japan, Belgium, Holland and France, and

CLASSIFICATION OF AURICULAS

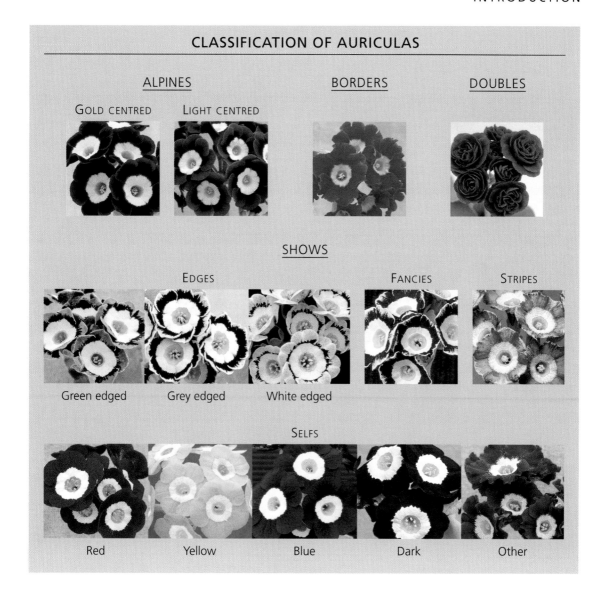

ALPINES

GOLD CENTRED   LIGHT CENTRED

BORDERS

DOUBLES

SHOWS

EDGES

FANCIES

STRIPES

Green edged   Grey edged   White edged

SELFS

Red   Yellow   Blue   Dark   Other

probably elsewhere, offering a range of these lovely plants. I have included a selection of the best-known auriculas from the USA, despite the fact that very few of these are available in the UK at present. The auricula is becoming an internationally known plant and is being grown anywhere where the climate is suitable. In many ways the barriers between different countries are being breached. In these days of instant communication we must not forget the

Internet: any grower with access can find information about auricula societies and nurseries very easily on the World Wide Web.

I must stress that the opinions expressed in this book are my own, and many excellent growers will no doubt disagree with them. The intention is to lay the foundations for the successful cultivation of these lovely plants, and to provide a sound basis on which the grower may build.

1

HISTORY

Primula auricula; one parent of the modern auricula

An auricula is a descendant of a natural cross between *Primula auricula* and *Primula hirsuta*, both members of the auriculastrum section. *Primula auricula* has yellow flowers, varying amounts of **farina** or meal (a waxy powder that can coat any part of the plant), and is often scented, while *Primula hirsuta* contains hirsutin, a strong pigment contributing red and blue – hence the wide range of colours possible in the hybrid auricula. It is also probable that other primulas from this section have contributed to the modern auricula,

Primula x pubescens 'Boothman's Variety' is closely related to *Primula hirsuta*, the other parent of the modern auricula

THE AURICULA is a primula. The primula genus is divided into many groups or sections, including candelabra, polyanthus and auricula (the auriculastrum section). The species within the auricula section tend to be very variable in nature, and hybridize with each other readily, especially where two species grow close to each other in the wild.

generally referred to simply as auriculas. In the wild it is unusual for *Primula auricula* and *Primula hirsuta* to grow near each other, as *P. auricula* is a lime lover and is only found in limestone areas while *P. hirsuta* prefers an acid (non-limey) soil. Occasionally, acid rocks adjoin limestone and where this happens, the hybrid *Primula* x *pubescens* may be found in a wide array of colours. There are areas with these conditions in the vicinity of Innsbruck.

In the sixteenth century, Professor Aicholz was given a number of plants that had been found growing in the Alps near Innsbruck. He then grew these in his garden where they were seen and admired by Clusius, botanist to Emperor Maximillian II of Austria.

Primula x *pubescens* 'Apple Blossom' has the same parentage as the auricula, but is a much smaller plant

HISTORY

Mid-1500s Auriculas grown in Viennese gardens

1570 onwards Flemish wool weavers settle in Norwich, Ipswich, Rochdale and Middleton, bringing their prized auriculas with them

1583 Clusius describes six varieties of auricula. (Clusius is the latinized form of Charles de l'Ecluse. His two publications are *Rariorum aliquot Stirpium per Pannoniam, Austriam et Vicinas* 1583, and *Opera Omnium Rariorum Plantarum Historia*, 1601)

1593 Clusius moves from Vienna to Leyden, probably taking his auriculas with him

1597 The earliest reference to auricula growing in Britain is made in John Gerard's *The Herball*, with the entry 'Most of them do grow in our London gardens'

1620–1685 Huguenot refugees begin to arrive in Britain (reaching a peak between 1670–1680), bringing auriculas with them

1708 J. C. Volckamer's *Nurnbergische Hesperides* is published. This contains descriptions of the writer's garden, including many fruits and flowers and a large collection of auriculas

1764 *The British Gardener's Director*, James Justice, mentions two main types of auricula – English and Liègeoise. The Liègeoise were described as self or plain coloured, many of which were velveted and shaded

1792 Publication of James Maddock's *The Florist's Directory*. This contained a list of auriculas, among them both selfs and shaded selfs, including some shaded selfs with continental names

1801 Publication of F. A. Kannegeisser's *Aurikel Flora*. This contained hand-painted illustrations of British and Continental auriculas identified by name, including Luiker auriculas (Luik is Flemish for Liège) which were shaded and had no meal

1809 Classes for selfs were included in York Florists' Society shows

1824 York includes a class for shaded selfs or Alpine auriculas; by 1830 Alpine (or shaded) auriculas are included at most shows

1873 The National Auricula Society is formed in the United Kingdom

'Holyrood' is an example of the sport that occurred about 250 years ago, when the outer part of the petal mutated to leaf

Consequently, Aicholz gave Clusius some of his auricula plants. Clusius took these to Leyden, and from there they travelled to the wealthy gardeners of England. It is thought that these few plants are the parents not only of the vast range of auriculas grown today, but also the group of primulas known as the *Primula pubescens* hybrids, which are like smaller versions of the auricula.

The subsequent distribution of auriculas is confused. The long-held view that the first auriculas were brought to Britain by Flemish weavers in the late sixteenth century, and also by Huguenots in the seventeenth century, is probably true to a certain degree. As these immigrants did not keep records and probably could not read or write, we are never likely to discover the complete truth, but this appears to be the only logical explanation for the concentration of auricula growers in specific areas of the country.

It seems likely that a parallel introduction into the stately homes and gardens of London also occurred. There is much evidence of the exchange of plants between English and Continental horticulturists, and the owners of large gardens were very keen on the introduction of new varieties.

The auricula is part of British heritage. Since its introduction to Britain in the late sixteenth century its popularity has waxed and waned. When times were hard, and during wars, their popularity diminished, while during times of peace and prosperity they flourished with many new varieties being **introduced** and listed. There have always been differences between the north and south of the country. In the north, the growing of auriculas had its roots in the working classes, whereas in the south it was often the hobby of professionals and landowners. Where nurserymen stocked auriculas they were incredibly expensive in comparison with today's prices.

The auricula of today is the result of many centuries of man's selection, in combination with a freak of nature giving the green-edge **mutation** of **petal** to leaf.

THE FLORISTS

An appreciation of the auricula is impossible without an understanding of the Florists and their history. In this context the word has nothing to do with the selling of cut flowers; originally a Florist was someone who grew plants solely for their decorative flowers and not for any other property, such as medicinal, that the plant might have.

The term is thought to have been first used around 1623. By the mid-seventeenth century carnations, ranunculus, anemone and tulips were all classed as Florists' flowers, and they were joined later in the century by the auricula. Over the next two centuries more flowers were added, and the hyacinth, polyanthus, pink, dahlia and chrysanthemum joined their hallowed ranks.

Florists' societies began to form around 1630, probably, in the first instance, as social gatherings. There are many references to the countless Florists' shows held throughout Britain over the next 100 years. The development of the Florists' societies and their shows did much to advance the cultivation of auriculas: the auricula had been accepted as a Florists' flower in the mid-seventeenth century and as such was widely shown by the numerous Florists' societies in the seventeenth and eighteenth centuries.

The Industrial Revolution (c. 1830–1860) caused a change in the working conditions of the poorer classes, bringing long hours in the factory instead of working at home on the loom. This reduction of time in the home led to a decline in the growing of auriculas and other Florists' flowers. Around the same time the wealthy growers, with their large gardens, were influenced by the natural style of gardening, as typified by the work of William Robinson and Gertrude Jekyll. This led to a general broadening of scope in private gardening, and the auricula lost favour with them as well. Another reason for the decline in auricula growing among the better-off was the increasing affordability of greenhouse heating, and the subsequent import of exotic flowers such as fuchsias and pelargoniums.

There was a revival of interest in auriculas in the 1870s, which could have been partly due to the development of the Alpine auricula. The growers of Lancashire and Yorkshire formed the National Auricula Society in 1873, and they held their first show in the same year, in Manchester. Three years later the Southern Section was formed, with James Douglas as one of the founder members. At a show held at the Crystal Palace in 1877 over 1,000 plants were exhibited, many of them seedlings.

THE TWENTIETH CENTURY

The success of the Crystal Palace exhibition fostered much interest in the auricula, and this continued until the First World War.

After the war, the societies were slow to recover and although there was an increase in breeding and showing in the interval between the wars, it was not until some years after the Second World War that the auricula became popular again. This is clearly demonstrated by the membership of the northern societies, which hovered around the 50 mark until the early 1950s.

THE NURSERYMEN

We can thank the House of Douglas and C. G. Haysom for maintaining stocks and introducing new varieties during the interwar period. The Douglases and C. G. Haysom were all commercial nurserymen with a love of the auricula, and their contribution demonstrates very forcibly the importance of commerce in both the breeding of new varieties and the maintenance of stocks.

THE BARTLEY NURSERY: H. DALRYMPLE AND C. G. HAYSOM

Mr Dalrymple ran a specialist nursery at Bartley, in the New Forest, Hampshire, England. When he and his manager, Cyril Haysom, became interested in auriculas, they soon realized that many of this plant's varieties were very poor and had lost their stamina. They proceeded to breed new auriculas, and the Bartley Auriculas were displayed on the show benches. The best of their seedlings were named and gradually distributed from the nursery, becoming much sought after.

On his death in 1946, Mr Dalrymple bequeathed the whole of his auricula stock to Cyril Haysom, who continued breeding and

'Walhampton' is a grey/white-edged Show auricula that was bred by C. G. Haysom, and named after a village in Hampshire

THE HOUSE OF DOUGLAS

James Douglas senior was a notable nurseryman and Florist. His collection of auriculas, developed from the late nineteenth century on, was considered to be the finest in Britain. The varieties **raised by** him and his son, James Douglas junior, and then later by his grandson, Gordon Douglas, have graced the show benches for 100 years, and still continue to do so.

James Douglas senior was born in 1837. He worked for many years in horticulture, during which time he exhibited a wide variety of plants, contributed to numerous gardening magazines, served on various Royal Horticultural Society committees, and was secretary to the Southern Section of the National Auricula and Primula Society.

In 1893 he moved to Edenside, Great Bookham, England, where he started his nursery, growing and breeding carnations and auriculas. His first catalogue, published in the autumn of 1893, included 82 varieties of auricula, many of which he had **bred** himself.

selling auriculas from Totton, near Southampton, England. These auriculas were named after places in or near the New Forest in Hampshire.

During this period, US gardeners became interested in auriculas, and imported many varieties from Cyril Haysom's nursery. Much of the US stocks are derived from these plants.

C. G. Haysom died in 1963, after many years devoted to the full-time growing and breeding of auriculas, along with judging and advising. He left a legacy of beautiful Show auriculas, some of which were to become the foundation of modern varieties and many of which are still grown today.

'Walhampton', for instance, is a parent of some of the top Show varieties of today, including 'Brookfield', 'Clare', 'Gavin Ward', 'Sharman's Cross' and 'Warwick'.

'Phyllis Douglas' is a beautiful Alpine auricula that was raised by James Douglas junior

Brenda Hyatt and her display of auriculas at the Chelsea Flower Show

His son, James Douglas junior, joined him in running the nursery when he returned from the Boer War. When James Douglas senior died in 1911, James Douglas junior took over the nursery (initially with his two sisters, but he bought their shares of the nursery within two years). His first catalogue was published in 1912/13, and included a picture of the auricula 'Phyllis Douglas', a variety still popular today.

He continued to grow and sell auriculas through the First World War until 1930 when his son, Gordon, joined the nursery after leaving school.

In 1939 Gordon left to fight in the Second World War and was away from the nursery for six years, during which time his father kept the nursery running. On Gordon's return James, then in his seventies, retired. Gordon embarked on an extensive programme to raise new auriculas and carried on the family tradition of exhibiting, winning many medals for his displays at Chelsea and at the Royal Horticultural Society shows at Vincent Square. The nursery continued at Edenside until 1967 when it was sold, but Gordon continued to run the business from his home at 67 Church Road until he retired in 1985.

BRENDA HYATT

On Gordon Douglas' retirement, his famous collection went into the capable and dedicated care of Brenda Hyatt, where it remains today.

Operating from a private address, Brenda has exhibited auriculas at Chelsea for many years, winning many prestigious awards and doing much to further the popularity of this plant amongst amateur growers.

Brenda has grown and loved auriculas for 30 years. In 1994 she was awarded the Veitch Memorial Medal by the Royal Horticultural Society for her work in promoting auriculas, and in saving old varieties which, without her help, could well have been lost. This she did with the aid of Dr Taylor of Wye College, using specialized tissue culture techniques.

THE PRIVATE GROWERS

A few British growers, Frank Faulkner in particular, managed to maintain some plants during the Second World War. These contributed to the new generation of plants which emerged over the next 20 years.

On browsing through the Auricula Society Journals of the last 50 years a pattern emerges. Between 1950 and 1970, a few new varieties appeared every year but the old favourites still won the majority of prizes at the shows.

During the 1950s, the major contributors of new varieties were Frank Faulkner with the Alpines 'Margaret Faulkner', 'Vulcan' and 'Winnifrid'; Dr Robert Newton with the Shows 'Jessica', 'Neat and Tidy' and 'Nocturne'; Fred Buckley with the Shows 'Chloë', 'Grey Friar' and 'Helena'; Jack Ballard with the Shows 'Serenity' and 'Spring Meadows'; and last but certainly not least, Thomas Meek with 'Teem', another Show.

The next decade saw Dr Robert Newton, Fred Buckley, Jack Ballard and Thomas Meek still busy introducing new varieties.

In the mid- to late 1960s Derek Telford, of Huddersfield, joined the Northern Section of the National Auricula and Primula Society. He won the R. H. Briggs Cup in 1969, with exhibits including 'Neat and Tidy' and many of his own seedlings. In 1972 Derek was awarded the Riddle Trophy for best Alpine for a stunning plant of 'Andrea Julie'.

Lovely new varieties from this talented grower continue to grace the show benches every year. He has won many prizes for his introductions over the last 30 years and the show bench inevitably includes varieties that

'Andrea Julie', a lovely gold-centred Alpine that was bred by Derek Telford

he has bred; these are mainly Alpines, but 'Oakes Blue', a Show self, is still the best blue available. And not only does he breed outstanding plants, he is always most generous in distributing them amongst other growers and to nurseries. The wide choice of auriculas available in the trade today would be a lot poorer without Derek's contributions.

THE MODERN AURICULA

By the mid-1980s a transformation had taken place and new auricula varieties contributed significantly to the show benches.

In the early 1980s, research in the field of micropropagation made it possible, under laboratory conditions, to produce thousands of identical plants from just a small piece of the original plant. This system had its drawbacks but it was instrumental in making a few varieties of auricula available to everyone, and this helped to increase the popularity of the plant.

THE BRITISH SCENE

It was not only Derek Telford hard at work breeding new varieties but also Hadfield, Kaye, Jacques and many more. The spirit of competition had really taken hold. In the Midlands a similar revolution was taking place with Ward, Baker and others producing outstanding new varieties.

The last 30 years have seen major strides forward in the development of the auricula, and there are many growers who have made significant progress in improving and perfecting this exacting plant. Their work has made the auricula what it is today. The contributions of the modern hybridizers will be discussed further in Introducing the Plants.

Do always remember that the varieties of auricula available are constantly changing. Old varieties (with some notable exceptions) are lost every year and many new varieties are introduced, not all of which will stand the tests of time.

THE NORTH AMERICAN SCENE

As early as 1955 a plant of 'Argus' won the best plant in show at the first national show of the American Primrose Society to be held in Tacoma. It was also at this show that Denna Snuffer's first new Double auriculas were exhibited.

The auricula continues to grow in popularity in both the United States and Canada. Many of the British auriculas have been imported and several American nurseries list them. While at present there are only eight American-raised auriculas in cultivation – and of these, only the lovely yellow self, 'Mary Zac', is grown in Britain – there will no doubt be more in the future. Maedythe Martin, ex-secretary of the American Primrose Society, is breeding stripes.

THE JAPANESE SCENE

Auriculas are now becoming more readily available in Japan. Considerable numbers have been imported, and at least one nursery is listing a selection.

THE EUROPEAN SCENE

In Europe auriculas are becoming more popular; there is certainly an increase in interest in the auricula, and there are dedicated growers all over Europe.

Auriculas are available from several of the European Alpine nurseries. Eleonore de Koning of the Netherlands is a collector, and lists over 50 British varieties. As with British nurseries, she has problems coping with the demand for greys, whites and greens. Monique Dronet of France also lists a good selection, and her auriculas may be seen on display at the Paris Spring Show.

'Mary Zac'; a striking yellow Show self, raised by Ivanel Agee in the USA

2

VIEWING AND BUYING AURICULAS

THE PROSPECTIVE grower will usually see his first auriculas at a spring flower show. The auricula is a plant that inspires love at first sight for many people: the perfection and symmetry of the Show and Alpine flowers has to be seen to be believed.

THE FLOWER SHOWS

At any spring flower show there will be displays of auriculas. Many British nurseries stage exhibits at the Chelsea Flower Show and the Harrogate Spring Flower Show.

At Chelsea there are no plants for sale, but you can often place orders or buy seed. These days you can usually find a few named auriculas for sale at any show held in spring. There are usually several nurseries offering a selection of auriculas at the Harrogate Spring Flower Show, an exhibit by The National Auricula and Primula Society (Northern Section) and sometimes a plant stall.

THE ROLE OF THE SOCIETIES

The various auricula societies all hold their own shows. At these you will see a dazzling array of beautifully presented auriculas, exhibited according to the rules of the particular society. Never forget that the auricula is a Florists' flower, and is specifically bred and grown for the beauty and perfection of its blooms.

It is recommended that any serious grower joins at least one auricula society. The American Primrose Society operates in the USA and there are three main Sections of

This display was staged by the Northern Section of The National Auricula and Primula Society at the Harrogate Spring Flower Show

Martin Nest Nurseries' display at the Harrogate Spring Flower Show in 1988, incorporating a selection of Show and Alpine auriculas

The National Auricula and Primula Society in Britain; each operates as a separate and independent organization. The societies' yearbooks are informative and interesting, and their shows will give you an insight into the range and beauty of this group of plants.

There are usually stalls at the shows selling plants that have been donated by members, and at these you may often find unusual and desirable varieties.

THE NATIONAL COLLECTIONS

In order for a collection of any plant to be accepted as worthy of National Collection status, the owner of the collection has to apply to the National Council for the Conservation of Plants and Gardens. The collection is then inspected and thoroughly vetted to ensure its suitability and merit. A National Collection belongs to the holder, who accepts certain

responsibilities as regards cataloguing and preserving older varieties. All British National Collections are open to view at the appropriate time of year (sometimes for a small charge), and it is well worth looking at these collections and talking to the holders.

As auriculas flower in Britain during April and May, that is the time to look round. If you wish to view a collection, do please phone the holder first. Many collections are owned by enthusiastic amateur growers who often have other commitments – work, family etc – and, while they are very happy to show and discuss their collection, it is only fair to arrange a mutually convenient time.

Even when the collection is owned by a professional nurseryman it is sensible to book your visit. It can be very disappointing to travel a long distance to see a collection only to find that the owners are exhibiting at a show and although the nursery is open, the collection is not.

Part of the spring display of the National Collection at Martin Nest Nurseries, featuring light- and gold-centred Alpines

The National Collection scheme has done a great deal to further the cause of the auricula, not only by helping to promote them, but also by helping to conserve old varieties.

It has also been instrumental in improving the cataloguing of the plants, as it is part of every collection holder's responsibilities to collect and collate as much information as possible about his chosen plants, including descriptions of colour and habit.

For an up-to-date list of the National Collections of auriculas in Britain, contact The Royal Horticultural Society.

SPECIALIST NURSERIES

A list of the main specialist auricula nurseries is given on page 176. In addition to specialist auricula nurseries, many alpine nurseries offer a selection of named auriculas.

Auriculas may be sold as rooted cuttings in plugs, as young plants in 5–6cm (2–2½in) pots, or as established plants of flowering size in 7cm (3in) pots. Some nurseries have lists of what is available, some will provide selections of their collection, and others will take orders to fill when a plant becomes available.

Sales plants in spring at a specialist alpine nursery

the customer cannot see the difference. Often the very small differences, a slightly rounder outline or a smoother **paste**, both of which can be influenced by growing techniques, may only be apparent to an experienced few.

AVAILABILITY

The availability and popularity of different auricula varieties is continuously evolving. New varieties are being bred and older (though sometimes not so old) varieties are losing their vigour and disappearing. For an up-to-date list of successful varieties, it is always worth studying the plants that have been exhibited at the auricula shows, the losers as well as the winners. These may be found in the societies' yearbooks.

Many novice collectors do not realize that certain auriculas reproduce very slowly and are thus very scarce. Nurserymen and growers cannot wave a magic wand and suddenly produce hundreds of a particularly sought-after plant. Unfortunately, just because you have seen two rare plants in a collection, it doesn't mean there will be a spare one for you.

Many growers who have bred a prizewinning new variety will only let plants go to experienced growers and I can certainly understand this; it is a form of insurance for the survival of that plant. If they inadvertently lose their plants they can then replace them from the other experienced grower. Also, in a few years, if the plant lives up to its early promise, there should be a good stock of that plant available for everyone.

Having said this, do remember that on the show bench there are as many readily obtainable auricula varieties winning prizes as there are rarities.

As there are only a few nurseries specializing in auriculas, it is often necessary to buy plants by mail order. It is sensible to first order just a few, so that you can assess the quality of the plants, and also that of the packing and delivery, before placing a large order with any one nursery.

Another wise precaution is to repot every new auricula introduced into your collection. Most nurserymen are very careful to ensure that their plants are pest free, but it is an almost impossible task to guarantee that every pot is without vine weevil. The modern chemicals used do provide some protection but they are not foolproof.

Occasionally you will purchase a plant that is obviously incorrectly named; do tell the nursery, as they can then remedy the situation. The most common cause of incorrect naming is customers taking labels out of pots to see which variety they are admiring, then putting the label back in the wrong pot. Of course, mistakes can happen when potting – while they try to be very careful, growers are only human. Some varieties are very similar and

3

CULTIVATION

URICULAS CAN be grown anywhere where the climate is temperate. This includes countries which have an average yearly rainfall of 50–150cm (20–60in) which, although spread over the whole year, can be more in one season than another, and an average monthly temperature ranging from 4–24°C (25–75°F). Temperate summers are classed as warm to hot, and temperate winters as cool to cold.

GARDEN VERSUS GREENHOUSE

There are auriculas suitable for many positions; the secret to success lies in choosing the types that will succeed in *your* garden.

It is no use trying to grow the Show varieties on a hot, sunny rockery. If you are determined to grow these aristocrats without a greenhouse you can, but you will have to use your ingenuity and common sense in order to provide the conditions that they need in order to flourish.

The auricula is perfectly hardy and can be grown in the garden given the right conditions, but I do recommend caution. If you wish to grow auriculas outside, try the Alpines first. Edges are more demanding than selfs and fancies, which in turn are more demanding than Alpines. A generalization I know, but it is sensible to learn to grow the Alpines, selfs and fancies before attempting the edges.

As an added caution, I would be loath to experiment with a single valuable plant; it would be far better to grow it on for a while, until there are some good offsets, and then try one of those outside.

IN THE COLD GREENHOUSE

ALPINE, BORDER, SHOW AND DOUBLE AURICULAS

This section also covers growing auriculas in polythene tunnels, cold frames, conservatories and large glass porches with a clear roof – in fact, any structure that will provide plenty of light and protection from rain.

The Florists' auriculas require overhead protection; a greenhouse with plenty of ventilation is ideal. By definition, a cold greenhouse is one that is unheated, but yes, they do get rather warm in the summer months, so shading is essential in the late spring and summer. Strong sun can be harmful to auriculas, but they are able to tolerate quite high temperatures in the shade.

Shading
While dependent on the weather, this is usually necessary from about mid-April to mid-September. Often shading is measured by a figure which denotes by how much the light is reduced. We find 50% shading is about right. The most common method of providing shading is to apply a special white paint – 'coolglass' paint, available commercially – to the roof, sides and ends of the greenhouse. This can be applied in the spring and rubbed or washed off in the autumn. Research into shading has shown that green shading cuts out some of the light which is beneficial to plants, and certain species are healthier when grown with white shading. We have not noticed any difference, and we use both types.

Alternative methods include shading with newspaper, teak roll-down blinds or green netting, which is a good modern material.

COMPOST FOR PLASTIC POTS	COMPOST FOR CLAY POTS
1 part John Innes No 2 (loam based)	8 parts John Innes No 2
1 part moss peat	1 part moss peat
1 part 6mm grit (washed)	1 part 6mm grit (washed)

Pots

I am often asked whether plastic or clay pots are better for the plant, and the answer is simple. Use whichever you feel happier with, but do use the appropriate compost. This is very important as clay pots lose moisture through the sides of the pot as well as the surface of the compost, whereas plastic pots only lose moisture from the surface. Auriculas are usually grown in 9 or 10cm (3½ or 4in) pots when mature, but don't over-pot young plants – 7cm (3in) is ample.

Composts

Every grower has his own opinions about composts; the old books describe some horrific mixtures which often contained assorted manures, including human. Some growers use peat-based compost very successfully but with this, you must take care not to over-water in winter or you will end up with no roots due to root rot (see Watering, page 24).

The composts recommended below are very basic and are intended only as a guideline; every grower needs to develop a compost to suit their own method of growing. With the correct watering they will produce a healthy plant with a good root system, but they won't produce show-quality flowers. In order to achieve show blooms, a sensible feeding regime must be developed.

Top dressing

On the show bench top dressing is frowned upon. The compost should be clean and unadorned. In my opinion top dressing can cause problems when growing auriculas. It is the practice to top dress alpine plants (such as saxifrages and androsaces) with grit, and growers will often do the same with auriculas. However, this prevents the compost from drying out which can cause waterlogging and consequent problems with root rot. It also prevents the grower from judging how much water to give the plant.

Feeding

I recommend that you start feeding when growth starts in the spring. Too much food can cause soft growth, which is more susceptible to disease. The tightly furled leaves of winter will start to unfurl, and the whole appearance of a plant will subtly change as growth starts – it will become a fresher green and more alive. The right time to start feeding depends on the weather – if it is still very cold and dark it is advisable to delay feeding. Different varieties need different food in order to grow to perfection. I like to use a half-strength balanced fertilizer, such as Phostrogen, once a week, but would add that the edges, from when the flower **truss** appears, need a feed higher in nitrogen to develop the edge fully. Auriculas like to 'search' for sustenance; this promotes root growth as in their natural mountain habitat.

Any newly potted plants, if they have an established root ball, will benefit from light feed once a week in September and October or until the weather starts getting cold.

Watering

In general I prefer to water from the top of the pot using a narrow-spouted watering can: as the water passes through the compost it pulls air down after it, and plant roots require air as well as water and food.

It can be very useful to stand the pots on capillary matting that has been covered with black, woven groundcover material. This, if kept moist, helps prevent the compost from becoming too dry.

Never leave the plants standing in saucers of water for any length of time: this can lead to waterlogging, and possibly consequent death. Standing the pots in water for a few minutes, however, is a perfectly acceptable method of watering.

Repotting

Auriculas need repotting every year, whether they are for showing or for your own pleasure. Repotting is normally done after flowering, though in the UK, some growers prefer to wait until June or even July. Propagation is usually done at the same time as potting, so refer to Chapter 4 and make sure you have everything you need before starting. Your repotting requirements are:

- enough clean pots
- labels and a pencil
- scissors
- compost
- flowers of sulphur (optional)
- hormone powder (optional)

WATERING THROUGH THE YEAR

March to June

Keep the plant moist, but beware of waterlogging – this is bad for auriculas at any time of year.

July and August

If very hot, keep watering to a minimum: if auriculas are in soggy compost in very hot weather, the roots will quickly rot. I have heard this referred to as 'stewing the roots off'. Even the most experienced grower can make this mistake. If you look at your auriculas on a very hot day and they are wilting, the automatic action is to connect the hosepipe and give them a really good soak. *Wrong.* As a temporary measure, give them extra shading (even material or newspaper laid directly on the plants) or move them to a cooler place. In the evening, when it is cooler, give each plant a small amount of water, say one dessertspoonful, and be very careful with the watering until the weather becomes cooler. If you find you have over-watered, try to

put the plants in a cooler place, keep the compost nearly, but not quite dry, and it is possible that new roots will grow.

As an emergency treatment, if you find a few waterlogged plants standing in a puddle, gently remove the plant from the pot and stand the whole plant on several thicknesses of newspaper for an hour or two. It is quite surprising how much excess water can be drawn out of the compost this way.

September

Water as necessary. The soil should be kept not too wet and not too dry.

October to February

Keep watering to the minimum. At all times be careful not to splash any water on the leaves and flowers as this will spoil the very attractive meal, and the marks may still be evident at flowering time.

METHOD FOR REPOTTING

1 Take the plant out of the pot, and remove *all* of the compost. This should be kept well away from the new compost and disposed of sensibly – seal it in plastic bags before placing it in the dustbin. If you are sure it contains no root aphids or vine weevil eggs, you can place it on your general garden compost heap.

2 Remove all dead or dying leaves.

3 Examine the roots and cut away any diseased or rotting sections.

4 Examine the **carrot**. This is the thick central stem that supports the leaves at the top, and from which the roots grow.

5 Cut away any surplus and/or diseased carrot. It is advisable to dust the cut surfaces with a fungicide such as **flowers of sulphur** to prevent disease entering the wound. Don't worry about the old roots that will be cut away with the carrot – there are plenty left.

6 Trim the remaining roots to a manageable length. I usually trim roots to the depth of the pot I will be repotting into. This encourages the plant to grow new roots and hence leads to better establishment.

7 Fill about half of the pot with compost, hold the pot nearly horizontal and lay the plant and roots on the compost. Holding the plant in the middle of the pot, gradually stand the pot upright while filling it to the top with compost. Firm very gently.

8 Label with name, date and any other details you require.

9 When you have potted and labelled, say 20–30 pots, water the plants in thoroughly – a full two-gallon can should be enough. I prefer to water in with a rose on the can.

10 Put the newly potted plants in a shaded place with plenty of fresh air, but not a howling gale or even a strong draught as this can cause dehydration (wilting) of the leaves. Stand the pots on a thin layer of sand or fine grit. This serves two purposes; the grit acts as a moisture reservoir, and it also helps draw surplus water from the pot.

11 Water as and when required. Do not let the plants become bone dry, but don't over-water them, as this can lead to root rot. The compost needs to be just moist.

After the compost has been removed from the roots, part of the carrot is cut off

The plant and remaining roots after part of the carrot has been removed

REMEMBER WHEN REPOTTING...

1 It is far easier if the plants that are to be repotted are on the dry side, but not too dry as that can stress the plant.

2 Work on one variety at a time, repotting and labelling all of your plants before starting on the next variety. It is very easy to mislabel plants and by the time an error comes to light it is too late.

3 While auriculas are very tolerant of root disturbance, on repotting it is sensible to water very thoroughly, then keep the plants almost dry until they are well established and showing signs of new growth.

4 All plants must be repotted into clean pots. Never re-use dirty pots; they must always be thoroughly cleaned first. As an additional safeguard, soaking pots in a dilute garden disinfectant after cleaning will help to keep disease at bay.

5 Make sure every plant is clearly labelled and replace any fading labels. Many of the so-called indelible pens are, in reality, far from indelible and will not last even one year without fading. Take care. An ordinary HB pencil does not fade as quickly, and is thus a lot safer.

A typical seed-grown *Primula* x *auricula*

Plunging

Plunging is only relevant if you are growing plants in clay pots. Following this method, the pots are sunk into a bed of sand to just below the rim. Theoretically, if the sand plunge bed is kept moist, the pots should not need watering during the winter months. This is supposedly better for the plants as the roots are kept at a more even temperature. I would add that the sand needs to be replaced or at least thoroughly soaked with insecticide at least once a year to prevent a build-up of pests and diseases, or am I being overly cautious?

IN THE GARDEN

PRIMULA AURICULA HYBRIDS

Primula x *auricula* may also be sold as *Auricula alpina*. There is a world of difference between the seed-grown *Primula auricula* hybrids and the named varieties. The seed-grown hybrids are easy, vigorous plants that will succeed in any reasonable garden and give you years of pleasure with minimal attention. They are available in a wide range of colours,

A small selection showing the wide range of colours available from seed-grown hybrids, *Primula* x *auricula*

so it is wise to select your plants when they are in flower. The range covers purples, reds, dark shades, yellows and even creamy whites, and the leaves may be plain green or with a dusting of farina (a white waxy powder that the plant exudes).

They prefer a good soil that is neither very dry in summer nor very wet in winter. For the best results the soil needs to be dug over thoroughly, and if you are in any doubt about your soil, dig in plenty of well-rotted garden compost or other humus-rich material.

If you are growing your own plants from seed, consult Chapter 4 to find the correct propagation methods.

Plants are usually purchased in 7cm (3in) pots. After gently removing the plant from its pot, unravel the roots and dig a hole deep enough to accommodate them. Next, position the plant in the hole, then backfill with the soil and water in thoroughly. Thereafter, check the plants every week or so – if the plants look healthy and the soil is not excessively dry, leave them well alone.

Maintenance

Every few years it is sensible to dig up large clumps, split them into several plants and replant as above. If you do not wish to split a large clump, but there is a great deal of bare stem, dig the plant up with a good quantity of soil on the rootball, put it to one side, then dig the hole deeper. Place the plant back in the hole, backfilling around the stems with the soil so that most of the stems are buried.

ALPINE, BORDER AND DOUBLE AURICULAS

These can be successfully grown in the garden, but are more particular about conditions than the seed-grown hybrids. They need a good, humus-rich soil that is neither waterlogged in winter nor very dry in summer, and light to medium shade in the summer months.

If you take care to provide the right conditions, the Borders, many of the Alpines, and some of the Doubles will thrive in the garden and delight you every spring with their perfume and colour.

'Broadwell Gold' is a lovely Border auricula that was discovered in a garden in Gloucestershire, England

Border auriculas thrived in old cottage gardens, but they were often sheltered from the sun in summer by the taller plants in the border, and the soil was much richer in humus than in today's gardens.

The named Alpine and Double auriculas have been bred for years to improve the quality and beauty of their flowers. As a result of this breeding they are unable to cope with the rigours of a hot, dry garden, so again, if you wish to grow them in your garden, you must be careful to give them the conditions that they require.

Maintenance

Maintenance for these plants is the same as for the *Primula auricula* hybrids. Unless you wish to save the seed it is advisable to deadhead the plants after flowering: this prevents the plant from wasting its resources in the production of seed, putting them instead to the better use of building up the plant.

The Alpine auricula 'Argus' growing in the author's garden

SHOW AURICULAS

We are often asked if one can grow the Show auriculas in the garden. It is certainly worth trying, especially with the easier varieties. Some of the more vigorous green fancies are very well suited.

Do also remember that the paste on the Shows will be ruined by rain if they are grown outside unprotected. If you are willing to tolerate this, you can still enjoy their beauty, they just won't be as perfect as they would be if they were grown under glass.

The Shows need a gritty, loamy soil containing some humus. It should be free-draining in winter but not arid in summer.

'Laverock Fancy', a green Show fancy, is worth trying in a shady place in the garden

They need light to medium shade in the summer months. One must remember that a position that is too hot and sunny can weaken the plant, making it less able to cope with the rigours of winter.

I know of one grower who grows his selfs very successfully in a trough outside, and another who has a border of green edges in the garden!

Maintenance

Check your Show auriculas regularly. Ensure that the plants are well anchored and look for any signs of attack by slugs, vine weevils, greenfly, whitefly or red spider mite.

The chief reason for constant attention is to halt any botrytis, to which auriculas are prone. This must be treated at an early stage. Remedial action usually entails scraping away the affected parts and treating with a fungicide, such as flowers of sulphur.

It would be sensible to split the plants every year, or at least every two years. If they become very congested it is possible for fungal diseases to gain a foothold in the dead and decaying leaves that become caught in the centre of the plant.

IN CONTAINERS

PRIMULA AURICULA HYBRIDS, BORDERS, ALPINES AND DOUBLES

These will all make a colourful, eye-catching display in the spring, but do remember that they cannot tolerate being sunbaked.

A suitable compost would be similar to that recommended for pots in the cold greenhouse (see page 23).

SHOW AURICULAS

If you don't have a cold greenhouse you can still grow many of the Show auriculas in a variety of ways, all you need is some imagination and a basic understanding of their requirements. These are:

❧ protection from excessive rain
❧ protection from the sun in summer
❧ repotting once a year
❧ suitable compost (I would recommend a similar compost to that used for plants in the cold greenhouse; see page 23)

Given a certain amount of care, many of the lovely Show auriculas can be displayed in containers while they are in flower. They will need overhead protection from rain in order to prevent any damage to the paste and meal on the flowers and leaves, but this can be fairly basic, for example, a sloping sheet of corrugated plastic. Or consider a cold frame with open sides, perhaps at table height.

Maintenance

Water regularly, keeping the compost just moist – avoid waterlogging. Feed when established. Renew compost and repot every year. In fact, maintenance for Show auriculas in containers is the same as that advised for maintenance in the cold greenhouse.

THE MODERN AURICULA THEATRE

An auricula theatre is a stage for auriculas. It is a lovely way to display your plants when they are in flower, and if you so desire, or require, having nowhere else to grow your plants, they can be grown this way for the whole year with a little care and forethought.

It may be a simple box structure with an open front and shelves, or it could be tiered, as seen at flower shows. These theatres are ideal for many small gardens, suitably positioned on a wall facing east to receive the morning sun. Stained wooden shelves are suitable, with an overhanging roof in one of the many man-made translucent plastics. Of course, it should be in keeping with the architecture of the house.

An auricula theatre in the garden at Calke Abbey, Derbyshire, England

THE AURICULA YEAR

Logically, the auricula year, in Britain, runs from June, when the young offsets are potted, to April/May, when the plants reward your 12 months' devotion with a glorious display of perfect blooms, and possibly some prizes from the show bench. Theoretically anyway!

If you intend to show seriously, and even if you don't, it would be sensible to keep a diary of what you do to which plants and when. Nothing is more annoying than experimenting with a new compost, and getting very good results, then not being able to remember exactly what it was. Brief notes on the weather are also useful, such as a very cold week in February, so the first major watering was delayed.

June

It is sensible to cut off the dead flower heads unless you wish to save the seed. If left on, the plant will put its energies into seed production rather than growth.

Removing the dead flower head

The flower heads should be cut off just below the flowers to reduce the risk of infection getting into the cut. This allows the stems to dry out and die off naturally; they will then come away from the plant easily. If the heads are cut off too low down the stems, moisture and disease can travel down the stem and cause the plant to rot. Cutting higher not only enables the stem to dry out, it also allows remedial action to be taken should an infection occur.

Many growers like to split and repot in June. Auriculas repotted in June will be good, strong plants by the following spring, and as long as a sensible feeding regime is followed, will provide you with top class flowering plants, worthy of any show bench. Other growers believe that early potting can lead to excessive autumn flowers, to the detriment of the spring display. Following this school of thought, they tend to repot later, in July or even early August.

Personally, I enjoy the autumn flush, and I have not noticed it reducing the spring display. The only thing that seems to reduce the spring display is lack of frosts in the winter, and this does not always seem to hold true.

July

Be ruled by the weather; if it turns very hot, follow the advice given for August.

SUMMER MAINTENANCE

We are often asked whether it is better to keep the auriculas in a shaded greenhouse or outside in the shade in the summer months. It is certainly cooler outside, but there is always the danger of forgetting to water, or alternatively of summer thunderstorms causing waterlogging. It would probably be good for the plants to be kept outside, after flowering, and until you are ready for the annual repotting. That at least gives you the opportunity of thoroughly cleaning out the greenhouse. I prefer to grow newly potted plants in the greenhouse, where the watering can be monitored more easily, but many growers do keep their plants outside all summer and into the autumn.

THE AURICULA YEAR (*cont.*)

August

Many species of primula go through a period of semi-dormancy during the hot summer months and the auricula is one of these. This dormancy is often indicated by the slowing of growth in mature plants.

August is one of the most dangerous months in the auricula's life. More plants are lost in this month than in any other, especially when the weather is very hot. Even in a shaded, well-ventilated greenhouse the temperature can rise alarmingly. If your plants are wilting seriously on a very hot day, either move them to a cooler place (even under the staging) or, if this is not feasible, spread sheets of newspaper over them. Leave them until the cool of late evening, then remove the paper and check each pot individually for dryness. If any pots are dust dry, give the plants no more than one dessertspoon of water.

At this time of year the lower (oldest) leaves start to yellow and often become blotchy. This is natural, somewhat akin to the leaves of trees turning colour in autumn before they fall. These discoloured leaves may be removed with a gentle sideways tug; if they don't come away easily leave well alone. Some authorities advocate cutting them off, but this leaves behind a small amount of leaf which could well rot and spread disease into neighbouring tissues.

The leaves that come away easily on pulling will already have formed a scar tissue on the part of the carrot to which they were attached. This scar tissue prevents disease from entering the plant.

September to October

As autumn approaches the auriculas come into growth once more and it is not uncommon for many of them to flower. This is known as the 'autumn flush'; don't worry about it, it is perfectly natural. However, some growers believe that it will lead to poorer flowering in the spring, so they remove the flower head (not the stalk). I prefer to enjoy the bonus.

The lower leaves continue to yellow and die. This process carries on all winter, and the yellow leaves may be removed.

November, December and January

During winter only minimal care is needed. Keep the greenhouse doors and windows open as much as possible. It is easier to keep the plants healthy when there is plenty of air circulating, and frost and subzero temperatures are good for them.

Check your plants thoroughly once a week, giving any that are very dry a small amount of water, and removing dead and dying leaves that come away easily. In winter I prefer to water early in the day,

The Double auricula 'Shalford', with leaves that have started to yellow

'Shalford' with the yellowing leaves removed. They have come away cleanly, leaving healthy scar tissue

WINTER PROTECTION

Frost is beneficial to auriculas and many growers believe that a cold winter with plenty of frosts will help the plants flower better the following spring. It is advisable to keep all the doors and windows in the greenhouse open to allow as much fresh air through as possible. The only exceptions to this practice are during times of high winds, because of the danger of damage to the glass, and thick fog, which can increase the risk of botrytis.

so that any water spilt on the leaves has time to dry off before night. Having said this, during periods with subzero temperatures day and night I tend to leave well alone, and delay any watering until the weather is milder.

February

It all depends on the weather. If it is mild you can start increasing the water, but do remember that the sooner the plant comes into growth the earlier it will flower. This is acceptable if you are growing the plants purely for your own enjoyment, but if you wish to exhibit at the flower shows, your plants may be past their best at show time.

Do remember that water spilt on the leaves will mark the very beautiful farina and make the plant less show worthy. The build-up of farina is a continuous process and to have perfectly mealed leaves, care needs to be taken from February on.

March

Spring is coming and your plants will now be in active growth. Some may even show signs of the first truss of flowers in the middle of the plant. Start your feeding programme, and be even more careful to avoid spilling water on the leaves.

April

From mid- to late April it will be necessary to provide shading for the plants, both to protect the flowers and to keep the temperature down. The timing depends on where you are; in Britain, the further north, the later the shading. It also depends on the weather. In a very hot, sunny spring, shading will be required earlier than in a dull, cold spring. As a general rule I would shade half the greenhouse two or more weeks before the show in your area. (In Britain, the Midland and West Section and the Southern Section of the National Auricula and Primula Society hold their shows in April and the Northern Section show is on the first Saturday in May.) This gives you the best of both worlds; you can move your plants about to hasten or slow down flowering if you are going to exhibit at the shows. The Alpines especially benefit from shading, as the flowers will remain attractive for longer. Direct sunlight does shorten the life of each bloom.

Pay close attention to watering, and don't forget the weekly feed.

May

Enjoy your remaining flowers, keep your plants well watered and fed, and start making plans for your repotting and propagating.

Careless watering can easily spoil the heavy meal on the leaves of the white-edged Show, 'Jack Stant'

4

PROPAGATION

ALMOST EVERY gardener wishes to increase their stock of a favourite plant, whether this be for their own use or to build a supply to give to friends. Auriculas are a good plant for this as they are easily propagated, either grown from seed or by vegetative propagation (taking offsets).

As all auriculas are hybrids and hybrids do not grow true from seed, the only method of increasing a named form of auricula is by taking offsets.

Plants grown from seed are invariably very different from the parent plant.

FROM SEED

COMMERCIAL SEED

Although auriculas do not breed true from seed, it is an excellent way to produce a good selection of plants, especially for growing in the garden. Seed available from seed firms produces very good plants for the garden, which will give you years of pleasure.

Garden centres keep their seed racks in a nice warm area where it is comfortable for the customers to browse. Unfortunately, this often means temperatures in excess of 20°C (70°F), which can cause any primula seed to go into

GROWING FROM SEED

Different growers have different procedures for growing from seed.
The method given below is the one that I like to follow.

1 Sow the seed in January, in a seed tray. Use a mixture of one-third John Innes seed compost, one-third grit and one-third moss peat, and spread the seed thinly on top. Add a sprinkling of grit, just enough to barely cover the seed, and water in thoroughly. The grit on the surface stops the seed from being washed into one corner of the tray in heavy rain.

2 Stand the seed tray outside where it may be exposed to the weather. Do not cover with glass or polythene. Check the tray regularly, and water daily if there is no rain. The little seedlings will appear within the next few months; leave them in the tray until they are sturdy plants, about 3cm (1in) across, and with several leaves.

3 The plants are now ready to be potted up. (Some growers will keep the plants in trays until they flower, removing and discarding any whose flowers indicate they are not worth keeping.) They are easier to handle if you allow the compost in the seed tray to become nearly dry. If you have enough room, pot the seedlings individually into 7cm (3in) pots. Water in thoroughly and stand on a thin layer of grit or sand. This will act as a moisture reservoir, and also help to draw surplus water from the pot. If you are short of space it may be better to prick out the seedlings into a deep seed tray or tomato box. Use the same compost as for repotting (1 part John Innes No 2, 1 part grit and 1 part moss peat or peat-based compost), and set the plants about 5cm (2in) apart.

Discarded as a seedling, 'Ling' was mistaken for a named variety, and stocks were built up and distributed

Even if they are not of show standard they will give you years of pleasure in the garden. Breeders of Show and Alpine auriculas raise many hundreds of seedlings with the seed coming from deliberate crosses (ie the **pollen** of one variety is placed on the **stigma** of another variety) and are very lucky if they raise one or two worthy of naming. Please remember that it is only permissible to name new auriculas when invited to do so, after the variety has won a class at an auricula show.

AFTERCARE
Keep watered, but not over-watered, until established. Do not discard the smaller, weaker seedlings: they often produce the most attractive flowers.

a state of permanent dormancy, and that means it may never germinate. I would advise you to buy your seed by mail order. There are several reputable seed companies that provide a mail-order service – they usually advertise in the gardening magazines from January onwards. You will find the seed listed under *Primula auricula* hybrids, *Auricula alpina*, and sometimes as *Primula pubescens*.

SEED COLLECTED FROM PLANTS
Propagating by seed from Show, Alpine, Border and Double auriculas is excellent once you realize that the chances of raising a good variety are slight. Having said that, there is a great deal of satisfaction in raising your own seedlings and growing them on till they flower.

BY SPLITTING
(VEGETATIVE PROPAGATION)

Mature auriculas can often be split to yield several plants. This is best done after flowering and before the end of summer, to enable the plant to establish before autumn and winter.

GARDEN PLANTS
After several years, garden auriculas will benefit from lifting and splitting. They can be split at almost any time of year, but it is safest in the early autumn. After lifting and splitting, the plants can be replanted in their new positions. At this time of year the soil is usually moist from the autumn rains and it is reasonably cool – newly planted auriculas need shade and moisture to re-establish; they will not succeed in hot, dry conditions.

It is advisable to dig over the area you are planting and incorporate plenty of well-rotted manure or garden compost: auriculas need a humus-rich soil to prosper. If neither is available, peat mixed with bonemeal or spent mushroom compost is better than nothing.

A healthy auricula ready for splitting

Removing all the compost makes pruning easier

AFTERCARE

If the weather turns dry and hot, water thoroughly once a week and make sure the plants are shaded from the sun.

POT-GROWN PLANTS
Removing offsets when repotting

Usually, any splitting should be done at the same time as repotting. (Refer to the section on repotting in Chapter 3, page 25.)

Auriculas are very easy to split once all of the compost has been removed from the roots (see the photos above).

Pot the young plants in the appropriate compost for the pot (see Chapter 3, page 23). Do not over-pot. This is defined as putting a plant with a small root system into a large pot.

To test what size pot is required for a particular plant, a rough guide is to hold the plant at the top of the pot, in the position that it would occupy if it were planted;

if several roots touch the sides and/or the bottom of the pot but do not look cramped, you have the right size pot.

Removing offsets without repotting

Offsets can be taken from the mother plant without taking it out of the pot. If you are using gritty, loamy compost and allow it to dry out, you can often pull the offset gently out of the pot without disturbing the main plant. Sometimes this will give you an offset without roots.

I find the easiest method to root one is to push it down the side of a pot of normal auricula compost and keep the compost only slightly damp. When it has sufficient roots, the offset can then be potted up.

AFTERCARE

After repotting auriculas – mature plants and offsets – it is very important to keep the

If there are excessive roots compared with rosettes of leaves, we prune the roots with sharp scissors

After trimming any excess roots, you can begin to split the plant and separate the offsets

The same auricula split into one large plant and four offsets

compost fairly dry after the first thorough watering in, watering only when necessary. This is essential until the auricula has a well-established root system. Many auriculas are lost because of over-watering after repotting. On the other hand, do not allow them to become bone dry for long periods: this can be just as fatal.

MICROPROPAGATION (MERISTEM OR TISSUE CULTURE)

A breakthrough in using the technique of micropropagation for auriculas came in the early 1980s, enabling many more people to grow and enjoy them. It had already been used for many years, very successfully, in propagating orchids.

Very simply, this is a method of propagation whereby a small part of a plant, under laboratory conditions, is made to multiply quickly to produce a large number of individual plants. The baby plants are then weaned to compost and grown on for sale. A wonderful advance when you realize that some auriculas may make only one offset a year, and others not even that. Another advantage of this method is that it reduces the incidence of virus, and appears to endow the plants with greater vigour. It is possible, by selecting the right part of a plant, to produce virus-free stock from infected material.

Initially, micropropagation seemed to be the answer to the problem of having a greater demand for auriculas than the supply, but over the years snags have materialized.

We have bought in two batches of micropropagated auriculas that had sported in culture. 'Marigold', that strangely coloured Double, had flowers that varied from pale lemon through to chocolate brown, perfect form, perfect leaves. These we sold as 'Marigold' sports. The other bad batch was

'Marigold' sported in micropropagation. The plant at the bottom of this photo is the sport

of 'C. G. Haysom' in which the meal varied from none to a very thick coating – these we disposed of.

I later discovered that this can happen if too many generations of micropropagated plants are produced, or if the laboratory conditions are not very strictly regulated. Such sporting is hardly surprising – we have so many different auriculas today because of their tendency to **sport**.

Since then we have not bought any more micropropagated auriculas, though they are still being micropropagated, especially any new varieties that are in great demand. I just hope a careful eye is being kept on them in case they do sport.

CONSERVATION

Although I am not happy with the use of micropropagation for the mass-production of auriculas, it does play a very important role in their conservation.

Dr Frank Taylor, at Wye College, has developed a method to reproduce auriculas from pieces of leaf, and this is being used to rescue old varieties in danger of extinction. The plants are carefully monitored to check that they have not sported in culture, and are only produced in small numbers. Brenda Hyatt has been instrumental in rescuing several old varieties and has supplied Dr Taylor with plant material from endangered auriculas.

It is important to conserve some of the old varieties, especially for the breeding of new ones. Breeding lines can become too narrow, and excessive inbreeding can concentrate undesirable traits in a plant and also lead to a deterioration of the plant's health.

5

SHOWING AND BREEDING

MANY GROWERS enjoy the thrill of exhibiting their plants in competition with other growers. The auricula presents a real challenge; it is not the easiest plant to bring to perfection for a certain date.

Obviously the plants must be in tip-top condition and have the requisite number of **pips**, but do remember what John Gibson (a grower of high repute) once said to me: 'It is the losers that make the show, not the winners'. It is not the spirit of showmanship to take only plants that you are sure will win. Not only are the growers competing, they are also putting on a display for both the general public and the other members of the society.

I have never shown auriculas seriously, but I have been to several shows, observed and listened, and the following notes are based on what I have seen, heard and read. I believe they provide a sound foundation for the beginner, but your own experience will always be the best tutor.

For plants to flower at the 'normal' time, they need to be repotted in June or July; any later than this can delay flowering and, unfortunately, influence the quality of the blooms, as the plant will not be fully established before winter.

Watering over winter tends to be minimal. The plants need to be kept in good health but they are in their dormant stage. Normally the grower would give the plants a thorough soak when the weather improves and the plants start to wake up. If the watering is kept to a minimum for a few weeks longer this can delay flowering.

Keeping the plants shaded and cool will also delay flowering. As mentioned in Chapter 3 (see page 22), shading half the greenhouse can give the grower the best of both worlds, and will enable them to move the plants about in order to get their plants in the best possible condition for the show date.

Some varieties flower later than others. Where this delay is very significant it has been noted in Introducing the Plants.

THE FLOWERING DATE

There are many factors that will influence the date of flowering, among them:

- weather
- date of potting
- date of first good watering in spring
- amount of shading
- variety

Of these, the weather is the most important and also, unfortunately, the one over which we have the least control.

INITIAL PREPARATION

As soon as the leaves start to unfurl in spring, it is time to start planning for the show. Separate the plants you are intending to prepare to show standard from the others in your collection. From now on take great care not to splash water on any mealed leaves as the marks will spoil the perfect appearance of the foliage at show time.

Give your show plants plenty of room; leaves rubbing against each other will also mar the foliage.

'Scipio' grown to show standard

'Scipio' grown by us, with no thinning or special care

WATERING

Water adequately and evenly; it's no use waterlogging the plant one day, then allowing it to wilt a week later. Do remember that different varieties will need different amounts, so check each plant as you water. The amount of water required will also depend on the weather; in cold weather the plants grow more slowly so will use less.

FEEDING THE PLANTS

These notes are guidelines only. As your experience increases you will develop your own feeding regimes.

Feed with a balanced fertilizer at half strength once a week, except for well-established Doubles which, being gross feeders, will need feeding twice weekly. When the edges and fancies are showing a good truss, say 5–10cm (2–4in) high, it is advisable to change the liquid fertilizer to one that is high in nitrogen.

Nitrogen is the component in plant food that improves the health and size of the leaves, and as the edge on auriculas is the same constitution as the leaves, this will help improve the size and quality of your flowers.

STAKING THE STEM

The flower stems on auriculas will often lean to one side, so when they have almost reached their full height it is advisable to stake them. The stakes can be split cane of 5mm (¼in) diameter, or even barbecue skewers. They need to be as inconspicuous a colour as possible, so as not to detract the eye from the flower. If they are plain wood, they can be carefully dyed to a less noticeable colour. Food colouring can be used, but do experiment first.

Tie the flower stem loosely to the stake. Wool is often used, as it is less likely to damage the stem, but again, you will need to find some in an unobtrusive shade of green. Specialist wool shops are usually very happy to help, but do take a piece of auricula stem with you: matching colour by memory is extremely difficult, if not impossible.

THINNING THE PIPS

The purpose of thinning is to produce a nicely balanced truss with 5–7 pips that all have room to open fully. If you wish to show your plants, thinning the pips is essential.

The process should be done gradually. Begin as soon as the buds start to swell, which is often before the stem has reached its full height. When you can reach the base of the **footstalk** the surplus pips can be removed using pointed tweezers or a small pair of scissors with long thin blades, such as those used in embroidery. It is usually advisable to remove the first pip, as on many varieties this can be much larger than the ensuing pips. Remember that the aim is to have them all fully open and flat at the same time, so the smaller buds will also need removing, as they will open a little later.

To present the most attractive appearance, wedge cotton wool behind the pips to stop them touching each other, and to enable them to flatten. This can be left in place until your last-minute preparation at the show.

PRE-SHOW PREPARATIONS

I cannot stress how important care in transportation is. It is heartbreaking to have the plants you have dedicated so much time and care to over the last few months ruined by carelessness in packing.

Beg, borrow or purchase suitable carriers for your plants. Any strong box can be used, cut down to size if necessary, and rolled-up

---

PRE-SHOW ADVICE

Check how many trays your vehicle will carry *and* that they can be wedged in securely.

Read the schedule carefully and make a list of which plants you are going to put in each class. There is nothing worse than staging your best plant in the wrong class because you were rushing, and seeing it given an NAS card (Not According to Schedule).

Make your plans well in advance, and make a list of the tools you will need to take with you (scissors, tweezers, cotton wool, paintbrush, methylated spirits – anything that will help dress the plant for the show bench).

Remove all dead and marked foliage. The odd spot on a mealed leaf can be made to look less obvious with the careful use of a dry soft brush. Practise on a non-show plant first.

Make sure that your pots, whether plastic or clay, are spotless. A dirty pot will lose you marks.

Practise preparing and dressing your plants on plants that you won't be exhibiting.

It is important that you arrive at the show venue early, rather than dashing in at the last minute thoroughly harassed: you will enjoy it more and your plants are more likely to win a prize.

PREPARATIONS AT THE SHOW

First, find a spare table for your plants, then collect your exhibitor's number and cards.

Remove any cotton wool that is separating the pips, then gently and carefully arrange them to best effect. Cotton wool buds or a matchstick can be used for this.

Make sure the leaves and flowers are clean. A soft brush can be used on the leaves of plants without farina. Any handling will spoil the appearance of a mealed flower, so great care must be taken in preparing it for the show bench. Some specks can be blown off, so a good pair of lungs is an advantage.

Specks of farina on the petals of selfs and greens can be carefully removed with a fine brush slightly moistened with alcohol (white spirit).

Arrange the petals of the Alpines to best advantage. Alpines are often arranged so that the edge of a petal is above the adjacent petal on one side and below the adjacent petal on the other side. Because of their shaded colouring, this is thought to improve their appearance. This does not have the same effect with the other auriculas, as their petals are not shaded. However, they are often arranged in this way to produce the flattened, circular appearance that is thought desirable.

Check that your pots are clean.

Read through the schedule once more to be sure that you are putting your plants in the appropriate class. If you are in any doubt, ask one of the show officials for guidance.

'Toot Toot Tootsie' groomed to show standard at Leeds, 1993. Note the careful arrangement of petals

newspapers provide very effective padding to prevent the plants touching each other. A trip to a local garden centre may solve the problem: they often throw away carrying trays that have holes of a suitable size. Remember, if the holes are close, you will only be able to put plants in alternate ones as the leaves must not be touching. Equally important, these trays will often need reinforcing as they are not made to carry large weights and could fold in half. A plywood sheet, cut 5cm (2in) larger all round than the tray, and with 5cm (2in) square beading pinned round the edge, will give sufficient strength.

PRESENTATION OF PLANTS

No grit or any other form of top dressing on the compost can be used. The surface should be unadorned, clean and weed free.

A single plant (one rosette of leaves without offsets) is exhibited, usually in a 9cm (3½in) pot. The leaves and truss should be in proportion and healthy in appearance.

The pips should be evenly distributed, not overlapping. Usually 5–7 pips, symmetrically arranged, are required.

Only **thrum-eyed** plants are allowed in the auricula and gold lace classes – **pin-eyed** plants will be disqualified.

The flower should be evenly rounded; the centre in Alpines and the ring of paste in selfs and edges should be even and circular.

In Alpines the shading should be even.

A single truss is judged. If the other truss needs to be kept on the plant it may be tied down. It is an old belief that the centre truss is inferior to one produced from the outside of the plant.

Some growers cut the centre truss off, thus leaving the plant to devote all of its energies to the second truss, but it would be a brave grower who cuts off a truss before viewing its intended replacement.

JUDGING

Please remember, the judge's decision is final. There will always be growers who feel cheated because they think their plant should have won first prize. Perhaps it should, but that is not the issue – judges are chosen to judge, which is what they do, and it is their opinion, and theirs only, that decides which are the better plants.

BREEDING NEW VARIETIES

Before embarking on an extensive breeding programme there are a few practicalities that must be considered, including what constraints you are working under – it is a waste of time and energy rearing 1,000 seedlings to then realize that you have neither the time nor the space to grow them on to flowering size. Do also remember that the breeding of a wonderful new auricula, superior to its predecessors, will possibly bring you fame, but certainly not fortune.

The mechanics of breeding new auriculas is fairly straightforward – the ripe pollen from one variety is transferred to the stigma (pin) of another variety. The first step is to choose your parents, remembering to take note of which characteristics interest you most. A lot of information can be gleaned from studying the parents of auriculas currently in cultivation; these have been included in Introducing the Plants wherever possible.

It is sound policy to choose the stronger of the two plants to be the seed bearer (mother) and the weaker to provide the pollen. Very carefully, using sharp, pointed scissors, cut away the petals and part of the **tube** of both plants so that you can see their stigmas. Using a fine artists' paintbrush, gently take the pollen off the **stamen** of the father plant. If it doesn't adhere to the paintbrush it probably isn't ready, so try another flower on that plant. Once you have gathered some pollen, transfer it to the stigma of the mother plant. When a stigma becomes sticky it is receptive to pollen. This usually occurs before the flower is fully open. If a stigma is receptive, the pollen will stick to it; you can check if it has with a magnifying glass. Repeat this process over several days, and at different times of the day, using several flowers on the mother plant. Tie a small piece of coloured wool securely, but not tightly, round the footstalk of every flower you pollinate to attach a separate label, similar to the example illustrated below, for each pollination. Note that the seed parent (mother) is always written first. HB pencil is the safest and most weatherproof marker.

It is also a good idea to record all of your crosses in a book with dates, times, and later, the number of seedlings produced. Then, the following year, add remarks about the quality of the seedlings when they first flower. The importance of keeping good records cannot be too strongly emphasized; you cannot improve on anything if you can't remember how and when you did it.

Carefully remove any pips on the plant that you do not pollinate and keep your parent plants watered and fed: all primulas are notorious for aborting their seed if under any stress. If the cross has been successful, the main stem will stay green and firm and the seed pod will start to swell. If it has failed, the stem will die away gradually.

In Britain the seed can be expected to ripen in July. Keep checking regularly; as soon as the seed pod starts to crack the seed will be ripe, and can be collected. It can be sown immediately, or sorted into small, brown paper envelopes, labelled, and kept in a container in the salad compartment of the fridge.

Sow the seed following the description given in Chapter 4 (see page 36). Seed sown immediately may well be big enough to prick out by September. For large seedlings an old tomato box is ideal, with the compost at least 5cm (2in) deep. Never discard the smaller seedlings: they could well be the show winners of the future. An ordinary seed tray will be big enough for them. For both small and large seedlings, use the compost recommended for plastic pots (see Chapter 3, page 23). If the seedlings are grown on through the winter in the greenhouse, many will flower the following spring and you can then start your selection. If you delay sowing until the spring it will be a further year before you see the results.

Once you have selected the promising seedlings, the remainder can be planted out or given away. Always grow a new seedling for two or three years: it may not live up to its initial promise – or it may improve.

There are seedling classes at all the auricula shows. If the judge considers your seedling worthy of a prize you will be invited to name it. Indiscriminate naming of seedlings is to be discouraged; there is too often a tendency to think your own seedlings are better than they really are. The independent opinion of the judge is far wiser and safer.

6

PESTS AND DISEASES

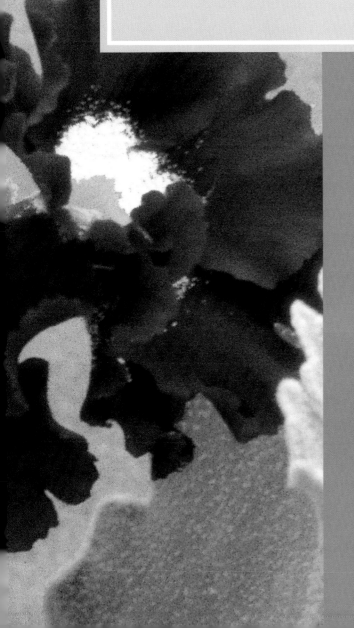

READING THE following list is enough to put a grower off auriculas for life, but do not be disheartened! In general the auricula suffers from far fewer problems than many other plants – this list is just following the principle that being forewarned enables you to be forearmed.

As far as possible I have avoided naming chemicals. The legislation regarding approved pesticides changes every year, as do the chemicals that are used to treat different pests and diseases. Any reputable garden centre will be able to offer advice once you have identified the problem; many will have charts identifying specific pests and diseases and recommending appropriate treatments.

A gathering of aphids and ants

APHIDS

DESCRIPTION
There are over 300 species of aphid; every gardener can recognize greenfly and blackfly, but these common pests can also be all shades of brown and beige.

Very rarely do they attack auriculas to any significant extent, but they do transmit viral diseases from one auricula to another.

PREVENTION
It is advisable to make sure that other plants in the vicinity are clear of this pest by using a suitable treatment or, if a plant is badly infected, by disposal.

CURE
There are a range of insecticides that are very effective, both **systemic** and **contact**.

BOTRYTIS, GREY MOULD AND FUNGAL DISEASES

DESCRIPTION
Mould and fungal diseases are usually a problem in very humid weather in autumn and winter, or if the plants are kept in an environment lacking a through draught of fresh air. The first sign is usually white 'mould' on dead and dying leaves. These are the fruiting bodies of the fungus which, once released into the air, will attack any damp and dying plant material. Drops of water that are

BENEFICIAL INSECTS

I have included this small section as it is not always realized that the following insects can control many pests and eliminate the need to resort to chemicals. Often a gardener will kill an insect they don't recognize because they fear it may damage their plants.

Ladybirds

Both the adult insect and its larva consume aphids (greenfly), but especially the larva, which most gardeners do not recognize.

Adult ladybird. These are black, yellow or red, all spotted

Ladybird larva (dark grey) and the in-between stage

Ground beetles and devil's coach-horse

It is believed that both these insects will attack and kill adult vine weevil.

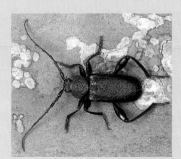

Violet ground beetle

Devil's coach-horse

Hoverflies and lacewings

The hoverfly looks like a slender wasp with its black-and-yellow stripes, but it flies in short, jerky movements, and hovers with quickly beating wings. The lacewing has a green body and large, clear, veined wings of up to 1cm (⅜in) across. Both consume large quantities of aphids.

Hoverflies on a flower head

Green lacewing

spilt in the centre of the plant can also become affected. I have found that it is the leaves with heavy farina that are most susceptible. Untreated, these diseases can quickly kill a plant. Once infected, a large plant with a small puddle of water in the centre can be lost within days.

PREVENTION
Plenty of fresh air. Plants grown outside are not a problem, and the following remarks do not apply to these, as the leaves will decay naturally with little or no danger to the plant.

In the greenhouse, the regular removal of dead and dying leaves is advised – say once a week. Always remove dead leaves gently with a sideways tug, and dispose of them carefully – not on the greenhouse floor. Keep an eye on leaves that were in contact with the diseased leaves, as a healthy leaf in contact with a rotting leaf can easily be infected.

CURE
Systemic fungicides. Some growers believe that these can distort the flower as it is developing within the furled bud of the dormant plant, but better a distorted flower than a dead plant.

CATERPILLARS

DESCRIPTION
It is usually the large, fat, green caterpillars of the cabbage white butterfly that are the culprits, and they are often exactly the same shade of green as the auricula leaves.

In a bad year they can cause havoc. They seem to develop a craving for auriculas and other primulas in August, and also occasionally in March and April. They chew irregular pieces out of the leaves and sometimes devour whole folded leaves in the centre of the plant.

PREVENTION
Keep butterflies out of the greenhouse by using netting over open doors and windows.

CURE
There are chemicals available to control caterpillars, either dusts or sprays, but hand picking is the best remedy and often the quickest as well; by the time you've been to the garden centre and found the appropriate chemical you could have removed the caterpillars from all your plants.

Cabbage white caterpillars enjoying a feast

CHLOROSIS

DESCRIPTION
A relatively rare problem. Excessive yellowing of the leaves, often in a fairly uniform manner and on the young as well as the old leaves, indicates an iron (or other mineral) deficiency which is called chlorosis. It is not to be confused with the normal yellowing that will occur on old leaves. It can weaken the plant and thus needs treating.

PREVENTION
Although auriculas like lime, it is sensible to aim for a fairly neutral compost. An excess of lime in the compost can cause chlorosis as the lime locks up the iron, making it unavailable to the plant.

CURE
Repot in more neutral compost, or treat with Sequestrene or a fertilizer that has extra iron.

RED SPIDER MITE

DESCRIPTION
This mite is not visible to the naked eye, but it can be seen with a 6X or 10X magnifying glass. It has a pale cream, almost transparent body with two brown dots. It thrives in hot, dry conditions, and can multiply at an alarming rate.

At one time red spider mite was only a problem in Britain in really hot summers, but with the increasingly hot weather we are experiencing in this country, it is becoming more common.

These mites feed by sucking the sap of the plant. Yellowing and blotching of the leaves and a general appearance of ill health will often indicate its presence. (Note: a yellowing of the outer leaves in summer and autumn is natural for auriculas.)

PREVENTION
Red spider mites do not like cool, humid conditions, so it is possible to deter them by regularly spraying with cold water or by keeping the plants in a cooler place, for instance, in a shady place in the garden.

CURE
Insecticide sprays.

ROOT APHIDS AND MEALY BUGS

DESCRIPTION
In my opinion this is often a symptom of under-watering. It always seems to be the neglected plant in a corner, in desperate need of repotting, that is affected.

Often the first sign of this pest is a white deposit on the side of the compost which you

This white, waxy powder is typical evidence of the presence of root aphids

can see when you knock a plant out of its pot. On removal of the old compost, you might also find the little aphids themselves. These pests will also congregate round the neck of the plant at soil level.

The damage is not immediately obvious. An infected plant may appear stunted and not be growing normally, but usually it will have become very badly infected before the problem becomes evident.

PREVENTION

Auriculas need repotting every year. If you wish to get the most enjoyment from your collection this is an absolute essential. Wherever your plants are stood, the area needs to be kept clean, as these pests will hide in sand, gravel etc, and enter a pot through the drainage holes. If you use a thin layer of sand to stand your plants on, it would be wise to replace it every year when you repot your collection. Evidence indicates a proportion of peat in the compost will help keep this pest at bay.

CURE

These aphids are waterproof; they are covered with a wax-like coat which protects them from sprays. In general, it would be better to remove all the old compost, thoroughly wash the roots, and repot in fresh compost. However, this is not always possible; where this can't be done, you need a systemic insecticide. This will be absorbed by the plant, and the aphid will then be poisoned next time it has a meal.

An example of healthy auricula roots

Auricula roots showing the first signs of rotting

ROOT ROT

DESCRIPTION
The plant suddenly starts to look unhealthy and will often have limp leaves even though the compost feels moist. The roots become brown and soft, not white and plump as they should be. Obviously, you will need to knock the plant out of the pot to notice this, and often the whole root system will have collapsed before any damage is noticed. The problem is most common in June and July, and many times it is the kind neighbour who looks after the plants when the grower is away who is responsible. I have heard of whole collections being lost in this way.

PREVENTION
This condition is usually the grower's own fault, due to over-watering. Root rot may even be a symptom of over-feeding.

CURE
If it is a problem, reduce watering and improve the drainage in the compost. You can do this by adding more grit. As a temporary measure, repot into grittier compost with less food, and cut away any diseased root and carrot to clean healthy tissue, treating the cut surfaces with flowers of sulphur.

SCIARID FLIES (FUNGUS GNATS)

DESCRIPTION
Tiny little black flies that rise quickly from the surface of the compost when disturbed. In the larval stage they are little, thin, semi-transparent white maggots.

On established plants the maggots do very little harm, and they are often to be found eating decaying carrots. On very young plants and seedlings, however, they do eat the roots and can cause a serious setback to the plant.

PREVENTION
Deal with this pest promptly as soon as the first signs are seen. It won't go away, it will just multiply to epidemic proportions. Clean your greenhouse out thoroughly once a year, making sure there are no dirty little corners where it can breed unnoticed. It loves moist, peaty compost.

CURE
Systemic insecticide watered into the pots.

SLUGS AND SNAILS

DESCRIPTION
These insidious pests need no description. Do remember that they come in all shapes and sizes, from the big black monsters down to the insignificant little brown ones that you can never find, but you know are around when a fine truss of flowers suddenly disappears overnight. They will eat leaves and even flowers, sometimes leaving a telltale trail of shiny slime in their tracks.

Remove slugs from your plants and garden as and when you see them

A snail just beginning its work

PREVENTION
Find and destroy the culprits before they wreak further damage.

CURE
The little blue slug pellets are very effective, as too are the liquid remedies. These may be used on sand and gravel standing beds, and seem to remain effective for quite a time.

VINE WEEVIL

DESCRIPTION
Vine weevils can produce a thousand or so eggs in a season and, as they only lay a few eggs in each pot, it is possible for one beetle to infest an entire collection. The adults are nocturnal, so if one beetle is seen, the chances are there will be more hiding in corners.

An affected plant doesn't look right. Given a gentle tug, the top of the plant will come out of the pot with 2–5cm (¾–2in) of roots. On closer investigation, white maggots with brown heads can be found in the pots, rapidly munching their way through the complete root system of the plant. If even, rounded notches have been eaten out of the edges of your leaves, it is highly likely that a vine weevil beetle is on the rampage.

PREVENTION
Prevention is always better than cure. As the mature beetles cannot fly, sticky traps on the bench legs are one way of stopping them reaching the plants. Scrupulous hygiene helps. Repotting towards the end of July, after the

The adult vine weevil

Assorted vine weevil maggots, including some in the first stages of the metamorphosis into beetles

eggs have been laid, and washing the roots can minimize the problem. Repotting any new plants introduced into your collection is sound policy, no matter where they come from.

CURE
Nematodes, used as a biological control, are effective where vine weevils are a problem, providing the instructions are followed closely. They need to be applied twice a year, once in May and again in late August or early September. They can be obtained from most garden centres.

Composts containing a systemic insecticide will provide some control, but as they are purely peat based they are not a suitable compost for auriculas, and need to be mixed with loam and grit. However, this dilutes the chemical making it less effective, if at all.

Recent research has shown that a preparation called Armillatox can be effective, if it is diluted according to instructions and watered into the pots at regular intervals. It is a moss killer, but has been found to kill vine weevil eggs as well. It also has a very strong smell that deters adult vine weevils from laying eggs in the pots. Unfortunately some growers dislike the smell.

VIRAL DISEASES

DESCRIPTION
There is a lot of talk about viral diseases but very little is known or understood. Auriculas do contain viruses, and these are transmittable by greenfly as well as by knives, scissors and other equipment used in propagation.

Blotching and excessive yellowing of the leaves is often attributed to a virus, but it can also be due to exposure to excessive sun and heat, or even the natural death of the leaves. Viruses rarely kill plants, but they can make them less healthy.

PREVENTION
Keep your plants pest free and sterilize your tools after each plant when propagating.

CURE
There is no cure. It is sensible to discard any plant that is badly infected. Micropropagation was said to reduce the incidence of viral infection, but the increased vigour of the micropropagated plants did not appear to last for that long.

WHITEFLY

DESCRIPTION
Small white insects that are usually found in warm greenhouses; fuchsias are particularly susceptible to whitefly.

Not a pest usually associated with auriculas, but with the recent hotter summers in Britain, there has been the occasional infestation. Whitefly are sap suckers, and will seriously weaken the plant. As they have a very short life cycle, they can build up into alarming numbers very quickly.

PREVENTION
Keep conditions as cool as possible, and dispose of any infected plants at once, placing them in a sealed plastic bag in the dustbin.

CURE
While they are resistant to many insecticides, a good garden centre may be able to suggest one. The best control is biological, and is obtainable from garden centres.

INTRODUCING THE PLANTS

THERE ARE over 2,000 named varieties of auricula in cultivation in Britain. **Hybridizers** continue to produce new varieties, and every year each auricula show has seedling classes; **raisers** of varieties that win these classes are invited to name them, so every year many new varieties emerge. Some of these will last for many years, others will disappear very quickly, and others will offset so slowly that they will only ever feature in a few private collections.

With the best will in the world, a list of auricula varieties can never be complete: new varieties are being bred every year, and old varieties are lost.

I have tried to compile a list of varieties that are available to the collector, and have used the *RHS Plant Finder* as a basis, adding a few of the newer varieties that the reader may be interested in learning about.

Please remember that it is often many years before a new variety becomes generally available. Some of the most sought after will only produce an offset every one or two years, and these are unlikely ever to be generally available. However, there are many easily obtained varieties that can be grown to show and prizewinning standard. You only have to look at the show results in the societies' yearbooks to confirm this.

The photographs in this directory are mainly of plants in our collection, and have not been grown to show standard. I apologize to the Florists, who no doubt will be disappointed that the illustrations are not of show-quality plants, but this book has been written for the beginner.

USING THIS DIRECTORY

I would strongly advise you not to use the photographs in an attempt to identify your own nameless plants – this leads to confusion. No matter how sure you are that your plant is the same as that in the photo, do not yield to temptation as it is highly unlikely to be the same variety.

Please note that the 'Date shown' is not necessarily the first date that a plant appeared on the show bench, nor does it indicate that the plant won a prize, just that the grower felt it was worthy of exhibiting. These dates were gleaned in an exhausting study of most of the Northern yearbooks (and some of the Southern, and Midland and West yearbooks) since 1950.

Please refer to Appendix II, page 173, for a table of the trophies and awards listed.

My apologies in advance for any varieties that should have been included but haven't been.

ALPINES

THE QUIET beauty of the Alpine auriculas is often overshadowed by the exotic appearance of the Show varieties, but they cannot be too highly recommended, either as plants for the cold greenhouse or for the garden.

ORIGINS

References to the Liégeoise auriculas began to appear around the middle of the eighteenth century. These were described as plain coloured and sometimes shaded. Towards the end of that century shaded auriculas were available in England, some of them with continental names. These came to be known as Alpine auriculas, a term not to be confused with the alpines that are rock plants.

The Alpine auricula, as it is known today, owes much to the work of Charles Turner of Slough (in Buckinghamshire, England) who

The gold-centred Alpine 'Gee Cross' has no farina on either the flowers or the leaves

raised many new varieties between 1861 and 1871. The Alpines were first shown in Manchester in 1873 at the inaugural show of the National Auricula Society. The Douglases of Great Bookham continued breeding Alpines, and some of their varieties are still popular today. Many more varieties have been bred in the last 50 years, and we can thank these dedicated hybridizers for the dazzling array of colours available today.

DESCRIPTION

Alpine auriculas are divided into gold- and light-centred varieties. The centre may be cream, white or gold. There is no ring of paste and no meal on either the flowers or the leaves. Some varieties may have meal on the

ALPINE AURICULAS

No circle of paste

Gold centred   Light centred

Petals evenly shaded; dark near centre, paler towards the outside margins

A selection of gold-centred Alpines showing the range of colours available

The flowers of the light-centred Alpines are predominantly reds, purples and blues

stem (which is classed as acceptable by the judges) and occasionally on the flower (which is considered detrimental). The petal colour should be darker near the centre, shading evenly to a paler shade at the petal edge.

Gold-centred Alpines have a rich gold centre and petals shaded in reds, browns, oranges and similar hues. Light-centred Alpines have a bold cream to white centre with petals shaded in reds, purples and blues.

RECOMMENDED VARIETIES

Gold centred

'Applecross'

'Merridale'

'Prince John'

'Sirius'

'Winnifrid'

'Merridale'

Light centred

'Adrian'

'Argus'

'Elsie May'

'Mark'

'Rowena'

'Sandra'

'Rowena'

GOLD CENTRED

'Aga Khan'

A fine, sturdy plant that is not difficult. It has red blooms with black shading. First listed by James Douglas in 1929.

'Alan'

A scarce variety, raised by Frank Faulkner in 1953 from seed off 'Tom Jones'. The flowers are shaded crimson-maroon to a lighter edge.

'Alison Jane'

Jim Sherwood raised this beautiful variety, shaded brown to gold, in 1972.

'Ancient Society'

This variety is in orange shades, slightly lighter than 'Piers Telford' (see page 72). Ken Bowser raised this 'Sirius' x 'Snooty Fox II' cross in 1991. It is named in honour of The Ancient Society of York Florists, the world's oldest gardening club, which dates back to before 1768.

'Andrea Julie'

A very bright plant, shaded in red to light orange. Raised by Derek Telford, in 1972, and named after his daughter. Only holds its best condition for a few days so timing is crucial if showing. It also has a tendency to flower on a short stem, so extra care is needed if exhibiting. (See photo on page 12.)

'Applecross'

A strong, vigorous variety that also shows well. Good red shades. Introduced by Mr D. Edwards in 1968, from seed from Jack Ballard. A 'Blossom' and 'Mrs Savory' cross. It is the sister plant to 'Sandwood Bay' (see page 73).

'Basuto'

A fine, vigorous plant raised by James Douglas, in 1935. Very bright and strongly shaded in crimson to rich bright pink. Exhibited in 1950.

'Blossom'

A beautifully shaded crimson variety, very reliable for showing. Bred from Douglas seed, in 1960, by Mrs S. E. Auker, known as Blossom to her friends. Exhibited in 1961.

'Bolero'

A superb orange-red variety which, alas, offsets slowly and is thus rarely available. Bred by C. F. Hill of Birmingham, England, in 1964, from a 'Bratley' x 'Shako' cross.

'Bookham Firefly'

Raised by James Douglas in 1936, this fine variety has certainly stood the test of time. The bright, well-defined centre contrasts well with the glowing crimson shading to a maroon edging. The truss can be irregular, but it offsets freely.

'Brenda's Choice'

This variety, raised by Arthur Delbridge in 1987, was grown from a seedling from 'Sirius'. The large flowers are maroon, lightly shaded to a narrow pink edge. Unfortunately the centre of this plant can be pentagonal. 'Brenda's Choice' was named after Brenda Hyatt, who expressed her admiration for it at a show.

'Bright Eyes'

A good variety bred by Derek Telford in 1983. The vividly coloured, small, flat flowers are shaded reddish brown to light brown.

'Brown Bess'

This striking gold-centred Alpine was bred by Hal Cohen, in 1963, from Haysom seed. The petals are strongly shaded brown to beige, giving a lovely distinctive flower. However, the petals of 'Brown Bess' do tend to bend backwards, which often makes it unsuitable for the show bench. (See photo on page 66.)

'Applecross'

'Basuto'

'Bookham Firefly'

'Brenda's Choice'

'Butterwick'

A lovely variety raised by Derek Salt, but not the easiest to keep in good health. Shades of rich brownish red.

'C. F. Hill'

Raised by Allan Hawkes in 1973, this striking plant was named in honour of his friend, Fred Hill, who was a leading hybridizer and raiser of Alpine auriculas. The petals are very strongly shaded brown to bright orange.

'Carole'

This variety was raised by Keith Ellerton in 1977. The pips are brown shading to orange. It was shown in 1980.

'Cranborne'

Dark red shades. Raised by A. Emlyn James in 1961, and shown in 1966.

'D. G. Hadfield'

A fairly new variety. Raised by Derek Telford in 1993, and named after the talented hybridizer David Hadfield. The pips are red shaded to pink, with a rich gold centre.

'Doreen Stephens'

The bright red shades of this variety contrast with its rich gold centre. Another lovely introduction by Derek Telford, raised in 1989 from a 'Blossom' and 'Andrea Julie' cross.

'Dusky Maiden'

A 'Sirius' seedling raised by Arthur Delbridge in 1988. The large flowers are shaded maroon-brown to a lighter purplish edge.

'Elizabeth Ann'

This plant is reputedly a good parent. It was bred by Jim Sherwood in 1974. The blooms, which are shaded very dark maroon to maroon-crimson, have a rich gold centre.

'Elsie'

A beautiful variety raised by Jack Allen in 1976. The flowers are shaded maroon to light brown, with a striking gold centre, and are very bright and showy. Unfortunately the petals tend to reflex, thus marring its performance on the show bench.

'Erica'

A strong plant that offsets well. It was raised from a 'Prince John' and 'Winnifrid' cross. It has rich velvet-crimson petals shading to light crimson, and a light gold centre. Bred by Gwen Baker.

'Finchfield'

This striking plant was bred by Gwen Baker in 1976

'Brown Bess'

from an 'Overdale' and 'Goldfinch' cross. The petals are strongly shaded from a bright, dark brown to light orange.

'Frank Faulkner'

A lovely variety raised by Frank Faulkner junior in 1951, from a 'Tom Jones' and 'Irene' cross. It has velvety petals of dark crimson shaded to lighter crimson, and a sturdy constitution. First shown in 1951, the true bright gold centre and brilliant colour caused a sensation.

'Galen'

Ron Cole, from Scunthorpe, England, raised this fine variety in 1970 and, being a chemist, named it after the first apothecary. Its parents are 'Forge' and 'Robin Hood'. The lovely dark orange-browns are only very lightly shaded, making it very distinct. It was shown in 1974.

'Gay Crusader'

A startlingly bright plant, bred by Les Kaye from 'Rodeo' and 'Andrea Julie' in 1982. It performs well on the show bench and was awarded the Faulkner Trophy in both 1984 and 1990. The flowers are

'Elsie'

'Erica'

'Frank Faulkner'

'Gay Crusader'

orange-red shaded to orange and the overall appearance is very bright and cheerful. 'Gay Crusader' was named after a Derby winner, as are most of Les' auriculas. (The Derby is an annual horse race in England, run since 1780.)

'Gee Cross'

John Gibson raised 'Gee Cross' in 1980. He named

it after the village near Manchester where the 1980 Northern Show was held, and where the plant was first exhibited. It has vivid, bright red flowers, which are only lightly shaded, and a rich gold centre (see photo on page 62).

'Gipsy'

An old variety that was first listed by James Douglas

in 1937 and which appeared on the show bench in 1957. It is shaded red to dark crimson.

'Golden Eagle'

A new variety from Derek Telford, in brown shades. Raised in the early 1990s.

'Golden Gleam'

An old and sought-after variety which is shaded from yellow to gold to mahogany-bronze. This sturdy plant was raised by Gordon Douglas in 1950 and shown in 1952.

'Goldwin'

Bright and shaded from brownish-red to light orange. This is a vigorous and easy variety that offsets well. It was bred by Allan Hawkes in 1980.

'Goldwin'

'Haughmond'

An attractive, vigorous plant, shaded rich dark red to light bright red. It was exhibited in 1983.

'Ida'

An attractive plant raised by Jack Ballard in 1965 from a 'Bratley' and 'Chestnut Brown' cross. First exhibited in 1966. It produces a good truss of beautifully shaded chestnut flowers.

'Indian Love Call'

Shaded in red and gold, this Alpine was raised by Derek Telford in the early 1990s.

'Inez de Pintado'

'Inez de Pintado' is another plant raised by Derek Telford in the early 1990s.

'Janie Hill'

On its day this variety can be superb. It was bred by C. F. Hill, in 1961, from 'Bratley' and 'Tally Ho', and was named after his granddaughter. The flowers are dark orange-red shaded to gold, sometimes spoiled by a dusting of meal on the centre.

'Jenny'

Raised by W. G. Elliott in 1968, with flowers shaded maroon to pale maroon. This variety appears to be losing its vigour.

'John Gledhill'

This is an attractive and vigorous plant that is easy to grow. It has small flowers that are shaded maroon to light maroon. 'John Gledhill' was exhibited in 1980.

'John Stewart'

An old and still vigorous variety with dark port to light wine-red flowers. 'John Stewart' was introduced by W. G. Elliott in 1968.

'Kim'

This is a fine plant of reasonable vigour. It was raised by Alec Stubbs of Grassington, North Yorkshire, England, in the 1970s, though he was better known for his outstanding work with the small European primulas, and was responsible for developing the Wharfedale Series. The flowers are very deep crimson (near black) shading to light crimson, contrasting with the rich gold centre.

'Haughmond'

'John Gledhill'

'John Stewart'

'Kim'

'Kingcup'

Classed as a good show plant, this has large, beautifully formed pips. It was raised by C. G. Haysom in 1944. It is not readily available nowadays but is still in existence.

'Landy'

An attractive plant, shaded in dark and light brown.

The name is an abbreviation of 'Orlando'. It was raised by Derek Telford in 1987 and at its first showing, at the Northern Show, won the Seedling Cup. (See photo on page 70.)

'Largo'

This fine gold centre was bred by Allan Hawkes, in 1971, from a 'Shako' and 'Verdi' cross. It is a superb variety, but offsets are rare so it is in very short supply and much sought-after. The flowers are shaded in rich browns.

'Lee Paul'

A striking variety, excellent for the show bench. Maroon-brown strongly shaded to dirty yellow. Derek Telford regards this lovely plant as the best he has ever raised. Bred from 'Sirius', it has a bright gold centre without corrugation, and very flat pips. There are some clones in circulation (suspected of being micropropagated) which have a deformed centre, but a good clone is one of the best Alpines available. Raised by Derek Telford, it won Premiers in 1990 and 1991.

'Lewis Telford'

A good variety, raised by Derek Telford in the 1980s. It is a 'Blossom' seedling and is similar to 'Blossom' but somewhat superior, with a much better habit. Shown in 1988.

'Ling'

Strongly shaded in rich red to light red. This fine variety was bred by Les Kaye in about 1985. It was one of a batch of seedlings that he gave to a friend (me) who, in their ignorance, thought it was a named variety, built up stocks and distributed it nationwide. The mistake only came to light several years later. The name was derived from a broken label 'SEED / LING', the first part having broken off and been lost. It says much for Les Kaye's ability as a breeder that his discarded seedling still managed to come in the winning entry in the class for six Alpine auriculas at the Southern Show in 1989.

'Mahmoud'

Raised by Les Kaye prior to 1993, the result of crossing 'Henbit' with 'Phil Drake'. This unique auricula is gold with a scarlet circle around the eye, with the gold of the edge almost exactly the same shade as that of the centre. It was awarded the Faulkner Trophy at Cheadle in 1993.

'Maureen Millward'

A fine variety that is still vigorous. It has maroon-

'Landy'

crimson petals strongly shaded to light crimson. Introduced by A. Millward in 1974, in which year it was first shown.

'Merridale'

A small-flowered plant, with very bright orange-brown strongly shaded to light orange. This excellent Alpine was raised by Gwen Baker, in 1977, from seed out of the same pod as 'Finchfield'. (The cross was 'Overdale' and 'Goldfinch'. 'Merridale' was exhibited in 1980.

'Mick'

Introduced by Derek Telford in 1989, and a winner as a seedling. Named after Derek's helper and friend. It has large reddish petals shading to a lighter colour, and very good form.

'Mink'

This reddish, shaded Alpine was raised by Jack Ballard from a 'Mrs Savory' and 'Blossom' cross, and was shown in 1972.

'Nickity'

Attractive, dull red shaded to lighter red. A very

'Lee Paul'

'Ling'

'Maureen Millward'

'Merridale'

distinctive plant raised by Cliff Timpson. 'Nickity' is a 'Sirius' seedling. (See photo over page.)

'Olton'

Crimson-brown strongly shaded to light orange. This striking Alpine was bred by Fred Edwards in 1965 from seed off 'Bratley'. It is named after a suburb of Birmingham, England.

'Overdale'

A good parent, with red shaded to deep reddish-brown petals. Raised by Ken Gould in 1962 and shown in 1968.

'Paleface'

An excellent new variety from Derek Telford, raised in 1993. Pretty and very striking, like a pale 'Sirius'.

'Nickity'

'Prince John'

'Piers Telford'

A fine variety, raised by Derek Telford in 1991, in attractive orange-brown shades.

'Prince John'

A very distinct variety, the flower presents a neat, circular outline, and the large gold centre contrasts with the edging, which is shaded maroon to light crimson. It is a reliable plant for the show bench, where it is often seen. One of the most important varieties from James Douglas, possibly raised as early as 1916. Still vigorous despite its age, and offsets are freely produced.

'Quality Chase'

This variety has a bright brownish-red margin shaded to gold. Raised by Jack Ballard in 1966 and shown in 1969. An excellent plant capable of winning a Premier Award, but unfortunately produces few offsets so is very scarce.

'Rene'

Well-shaped flowers of rich crimson, lightly shaded. Raised by Jack Ballard and seen on the show bench in 1970. Easy and vigorous.

'Rodeo'

C. F. Hill bred this very bright orange-brown shaded Alpine from 'Mrs E. Goodman' and 'Verdi' seed. It was shown in 1965. On its day it is a good show plant. Unfortunately the petals are not always flat, but it is worth growing for its bright colouring.

'Rondo'

An attractive plant, raised by Allan Hawkes in 1969.

'Roy Keane'

A relatively new variety bred by Keith Leeming in 1994, with pips shaded purple-brown to orange.

'Ryecroft'

A strong plant with flowers shaded light dull crimson to dark crimson. Raised by K. Ellerton from 'Blossom' and 'Prince John' seed. Exhibited in 1983.

'Saint Elmo'

A startlingly beautiful variety. The small flowers are of near perfect form, and shaded dark red to light orange red. It tends to need thinning to show well. Raised by Allan Hawkes around 1973.

'Rodeo'

'Saint Elmo'

'Shotley'

'Sirius'

'Sam Hunter'

Bred by Derek Telford and named after his Ulster colleague. Shaded red blooms. Shown in 1988.

'Sandwood Bay'

Flamboyant, easy and vigorous, and it will even perform well on the show bench. The blooms are shaded rich red to bright orange-red, with a vivid gold centre. Raised by D. Edwards in 1968 from a cross by Jack Ballard ('Blossom' and 'Mrs Savory'), the seedlings of which were given to Dennis Edwards. Sister plant to 'Applecross' (see page 64).

'Shako'

An important parent that was raised by C. F. Hill, in 1964, from 'Rodeo' seed.

'Shergold'

Very dark red to golden-brown shades. An attractive and easy plant raised by Allan Hawkes in 1979, and shown in 1981.

'Shotley'

Another plant bred by Derek Telford, with distinct flowers shaded from brown-red to light brown-red. Exhibited in 1981. (See photo on page 73.)

'Sirbol'

A pleasant, sandy brown Alpine raised in 1990 and released in error. Not of show standard. The name is a combination of 'Sirius' and 'Bolero'.

'Sirius'

A strikingly beautiful plant raised by Frank Jacques in 1979. The blooms of maroon-purple shaded to cream are very bright and distinctive. An easy plant that offsets freely. Regularly seen on the show bench. (See photo on page 73.)

'Snooty Fox II'

Vivid orange-red, lightly shaded blooms. An excellent variety bred by Derek Telford in 1978 from 'Andrea Julie' seed. 'Snooty Fox II' is named after a pub in Solihull close to the Midlands Show venue.

'Sumo'

Attractive gold to dark brown shades, raised by Derek Telford in 1993.

'Tally-ho'

A good gold-centred Alpine, shaded orange-brown. Bred by C. F. Hill about 1959. The parent of several modern varieties.

'Tarantella'

This eye-catching variety is very strongly shaded in reddish browns. Raised by Derek Telford around 1982, it is the sister plant to 'Snooty Fox II' (see above). Exhibited in 1982.

'Snooty Fox II'

'Ted Roberts'

The dark petals, very lightly shaded maroon to crimson, contrast well with the vivid gold centre. It was introduced by J. Allen in 1977 and shown in 1981. For exhibition purposes it is advisable to thin the flower buds.

'Toffee Crisp'

A lovely variety introduced by Ken Bowser in 1994. The name describes the colour.

'Tumbledown'

Another from Derek Telford, this one in red shades.

'Typhoon'

An Alpine of dark, sombre colouring, shaded maroon-purple to dark purple-black. Raised by Arthur Delbridge in 1991 from 'Largo' seed.

'Uncle Arthur'

This richly coloured Alpine was raised by Tim Coop, who named it after Arthur Delbridge. The brown to red shades contrast with the gold centre. It was exhibited in 1988.

'Tarantella'

'Ted Roberts'

'Verdi'

'Winnifrid'

'Verdi'

This very fine variety was introduced by H. S. Lennie in 1943. It produces a classical flower, flat and well proportioned, in reddish brown shading to a narrow edge of lighter golden brown. Careful growing is needed to produce a show specimen, as it seems to be losing its vigour.

'Winnifrid'

This lightly shaded variety was bred by Frank Faulkner in 1950 and was exhibited in 1952. It has lovely rich red flowers that always show to advantage. It is not to be confused with the Border auricula, 'Winifred', of similar name but different appearance (see description on page 99).

LIGHT CENTRED

'Adrian'

An excellent variety with neat, pointed leaves. It has blooms shaded from very bright purple to light purple-blue. Offsets freely and is good for showing. Raised by Arthur Delbridge in 1971, its parents being 'Gordon Douglas' and 'Frank Crosland'. First shown at Harborne in 1972, winning a First.

'Alansford'

A rich purple, lightly shaded variety that was introduced by Derek Telford in 1974 and exhibited in the same year.

'Alicia'

Robust and unusual – purple-mauve shaded to pink. Raised by Len Bailey, in 1979, from a 'Frank Crosland' and 'Joy' cross. Named after Dora Bailey's sister.

'Andrew Hunter'

Derek Telford raised this lovely sister to 'Avril Hunter' (see above right), shaded in purple, in 1990.

'Ann Taylor'

A pure white centre, round, true and clean, sets off the strongly shaded, light blue petals. This plant is very early flowering and not the easiest variety to grow well. Raised by Bob Taylor in 1979, from blue Alpine seed from the House of Douglas, and named after his wife. Won the Premier Alpine Award at Cheadle in 1985.

'Anwar Sadat'

Derek Telford raised this good variety, strongly shaded in blue to mauve, in 1988. Named after President Sadat of Egypt.

'Argus'

An excellent white-centred variety, in shades of crimson-red. It was bred around 1890 by J. J. Keen of Southampton, England. Still wins top prizes when grown well.

'Aurora'

James Douglas raised this variety, strongly shaded in crimson to bright rich pink. It was exhibited in 1962.

'Avril Hunter'

A lovely variety, strongly shaded in dark purple-blue to light blue. Raised by Derek Telford in 1988. (See photo on page 78.)

'Beatrice'

Not of great merit for the show bench, but a lovely variety nonetheless. Strongly shaded in blue to light blue. Raised by James Douglas in 1914. (See photo on page 78.)

'Blue Bonnet'

A fine old variety in medium blue shades. Bred by James Douglas. First listed in 1926.

'C. W. Needham'

A lovely plant raised in 1934 by Percy Johnson, from Hale in Cheshire, England. It has distinctive, evenly serrated leaves and the petals are lightly shaded dark blue tending to purple; the colour can vary depending on the amount of shading and feeding. (See photo on page 79.)

'Chelsea Bridge'

A small plant with blooms strongly shaded in purple-blue.

'Cherry Picker'

A fairly old variety, exhibited in 1964. The petals are shaded crimson to pink.

'Cicero'

Despite messy leaves, this large-flowered variety can produce an excellent truss, evenly shaded in purple-blue, from light to dark. Raised by Les Kaye in 1981.

'Adrian'

'Alansford'

'Anwar Sadat'

'Argus'

'Comet'

'Comet' is yet another of Derek Telford's excellent Alpines. This light-centred variety was raised around 1980 and was first shown in 1983. It is similar to J. J. Keen's 'Argus' (see description on page 76 and photo above), with flowers that are shaded from vivid pink to crimson, with a very pale centre. 'Comet' is a good, reliable plant, making it ideal for the garden.

'Connaught Court'

A dark pink, after the style of 'Mark'. Raised by Derek Telford in 1995. (See description on page 84.)

'Craig Vaughan'

One of the older varieties, the cream centre contrasts well with the velvety purple, shaded petals. It was exhibited in 1971.

'Avril Hunter'

'Beatrice'

'Crecy'

A very pretty and distinct plant, this free-flowering variety has small flowers and is strongly shaded from light pink to dark crimson. It was raised by Derek Telford in 1995.

'Diane'

The dark, velvety crimson, lightly shaded flowers of this variety contrast beautifully with its very pale cream centre. It was raised by Jack Allen from Partington, in Manchester, England, in about 1978 and exhibited in 1983. It is a similar plant to 'Argus' (see description on page 76 and photo on page 77).

'Divint Dunch'

The medium-sized flowers are plum purple shading to light pinky mauve. This variety was raised by Derek Telford in 1990. Roughly translated from the Geordie (a dialect spoken in Newcastle, England), the name means 'don't push'.

'Donhead'

An older Alpine with flowers shaded in wine red. This variety was raised by A. Emlyn James in 1966 and shown in 1967.

'Doris Jean'

Frank Jacques raised this distinct plant around 1975, from a 'Rowena' and 'Peggy' cross, and named it after his wife. It was first exhibited in 1975 where it was awarded a Premier. The flowers are shaded pink to dark pink to dark crimson-red.

'Douglas Bader'

A new variety in blue shades, raised by Derek Telford in 1995.

'Ellen Thompson'

An old variety, in shades of blue, that was raised by J. Robinson and exhibited in 1961.

'Elsie May'

The flowers are a deep plum purple shading to purplish pink. Bred by Derek Telford in 1972 and named after his mother. 'Elsie May' is a good variety for the show bench, often winning prizes. (See photo on page 81.)

'Eve Guest'

A very attractive variety raised by Allan Hawkes, in 1970, from a 'Roxburgh' and 'Lady Daresbury' cross. The flowers are shaded light to dark blue.

'C. W. Needham'

'Comet'

'Crecy'

'Diane'

'Fairy'

An old variety with purple to heliotrope pink flowers. Raised by James Douglas prior to 1939.

'Frank Crosland'

The large flowers are strongly shaded from dark blue through to pale blue. A justifiably popular variety that was raised by C. F. Faulkner around 1930. It offsets freely but can be short-lived. (See photo on page 80.)

'Fred Livesley'

Similar to 'C. W. Needham' (see description on page 76 and photo above) only better, and with a pure white centre. This fine plant was raised by Les Allen in 1994, and named after his wife's father.

79

'Frank Crosland'

'Elsie May'

'Gwen'

'Hermia'

'Ibis'

'Geordie'

Violet shaded to pale blue with a cream centre. Exhibited in 1986, this variety can be best described as an improved 'Gordon Douglas'. It was raised by Derek Telford and named after his brother-in-law.

'Good Report'

Raised by Derek Telford in 1992; in blue shades.

'Gordon Douglas'

'Gordon Douglas' has a flower of deep violet-blue shaded to pale blue, with a creamy white centre. It is a variety that benefits from being kept in a shaded position. Although it seems to have lost much of its vigour, being an older variety, it is still well worth persevering with. It was raised by James Douglas, in 1918, from a 'Roxburgh' and 'Mrs Berkeley' cross.

'Gorey'

A Derek Telford introduction, in purple shades, named after a holiday resort in the Channel Isles.

'Gwen'

This variety is a small-flowered plant that will produce a good truss. The flowers are strongly shaded in purple to pale purple. Distinct and very attractive. Raised by Allan Hawkes and shown in 1971. (See photo on page 81.)

'Heady'

Yet another plant from Derek Telford, raised in 1994. It is shaded in light pinks.

'Hermia'

This variety is rarely obtainable and seems to have lost its vigour. However, it is an outstandingly beautiful plant with flowers of dark purple strongly shaded to pale cream. (See photo on page 81.)

'Ibis'

The blooms of this plant are strongly shaded in pink to very dark crimson. 'Ibis' is an old variety that is still vigorous and offsets reasonably freely. (See photo on page 81.)

'Jeannie Telford'

This variety, with large flowers shaded from wine red to pink, is similar to 'Lisa' (see photo on page 84). Bred by Derek Telford in 1977, and named after his wife. It is an excellent variety for showing.

'Joanne'

This plant, raised by J. C. Bell in 1971, is in shades of purple and blue.

'John Wayne'

One of the top show varieties. The beautiful, pale pink flowers are evenly shaded to crimson. It was bred by Len Bailey in 1978/79 from a 'Frank Crosland' and 'Joy' cross.

'Joy'

An old variety that has certainly stood the test of time – after 60 years it still regularly wins prizes on the show bench. The rich, velvety crimson flowers are delicately shaded and contrast well with the clean cream centre. 'Joy' was raised by Percy Johnson in 1931.

'Joyce'

An old variety, raised by J. Baxter in 1969. The flowers are purple shaded to light blue. Unfortunately, as with many older varieties, it appears to be losing its vigour.

'Kelso'

This plant has flowers in purple shades. It was bred by James Douglas prior to 1936.

'Kerkup'

This plant produces a good truss of pips, which are rich purple shaded to light mauve. It was raised by Derek Telford in 1968. 'Kerkup' was shown in 1972.

'Kevin Keegan'

'Kevin Keegan' was raised in 1983 by Derek Telford and named after the famous English footballer. It is a lovely variety with petals of crimson shading to pink, and a very white centre.

'Kintail'

A classic variety that has often been used in breeding. The flowers are shaded from deep violet to heliotrope. It was raised by James Douglas in 1936 and has been seen on the show benches as recently as 1986.

'Lady Daresbury'

A lovely old variety bred by C. F. Faulkner at Hale in Cheshire, England. The large, well-formed flowers are strongly shaded in rich wine red to pale pink, with good white centres. There are usually eight petals. 'Lady Daresbury' was raised from the same cross as 'Peggy'.

'Joy'

'Kerkup'

'Lady Daresbury'

'Lee'

'Lee'

Attractive, and not grown as often as it deserves. Very strongly shaded in purple to light purple-blue. Raised by Derek Telford, and first shown in 1980.

'Lisa'

A lovely and reliable variety. It was bred by Derek Telford in 1978 and shown in 1981. The flowers are

strongly shaded in wine to pink. This plant offsets freely, and often graces the show bench. It was named after Derek Telford's granddaughter. (See photo over page.)

'Margaret Faulkner'

Delicately shaded in crimson-purple, this plant is a classic for showing. It was raised by Frank Faulkner,

'Lisa'

'Margaret Faulkner'

in 1953, from a 'Joy' and 'Gordon Douglas' cross. 'Margaret Faulkner' was first shown in 1954.

'Mark'

Another of Derek Telford's introductions, from a 'Thetis' and 'Rowena' cross. This variety has very large flowers, strongly shaded from wine purple to pink. A marvellous plant for the show bench when grown well.

'May'

An unusual colour, shaded in fuchsia pinks, sometimes spoilt by a star-shaped centre. It was raised by Arthur Delbridge in the 1970s, and named after his wife.

'Milkmaid'

Dark to light blue shades. Raised by James Douglas prior to 1931.

'Millicent'

A striking plant which is shaded deep to pale mauve-blue. Raised by R. Barter in 1985.

'Miriam'

This variety was raised by Jack Allen in 1977. The flowers are in blue shades.

'Monica'

Flowers in purple-mauve shades. This variety was raised by Ken Whorton in 1972 from an 'Argus' and 'Mrs L. Hearne' cross.

'Mrs L. Hearne'

The small, well-shaped flowers are shaded grey-blue to darker blue, with a pale cream centre. This is another fine Alpine, raised by James Douglas in the 1930s. Douglas first listed it in 1937, and it has graced the show bench for many years. 'Mrs L. Hearne' is scented.

'Norah'

Raised by R. G. Rossiter. Flowers in blue shades.

'Norma'

Shaded dark purple to light purple. Raised by Keith Ellerton, and shown in 1975.

'Mark'

'Millicent'

'Mrs L. Hearne'

'Pippin'

'Paragon'

An old variety in shades of mauve to plum purple. 'Paragon' was raised by H. E. Burbridge in 1952 and shown in 1954.

'Pauline'

This variety, in purple shades, was shown in 1983.

'Peggy'

'Peggy' is a classic light-centred Alpine. An older variety, it was raised by C. F. Faulkner in 1930. It is similar to 'Lady Daresbury' (see photo on page 83), with flowers in purple shades. 'Peggy' is of the same parentage, but does tend to flower slightly earlier than 'Lady Daresbury'. Seen on the show bench in 1950.

'Rabley Heath'

'Rose Kaye'

'Phyllis Douglas'

'Phyllis Douglas' has beautifully formed flowers, in purple-blue shades. It is an old variety, raised by James Douglas senior in 1909. It does tend to be early flowering, but grown well it is an excellent variety for exhibiting. 'Phyllis Douglas' is reasonably vigorous and quite liberal with its offsets. (See photo on page 10.)

'Pink Lady'

This variety has a very shapely truss, with pips shaded from wine to rose pink. Raised by James Douglas prior to 1939.

'Pippin'

The large flowers are shaded maroon-red to light crimson-red. The centre tends to be almost yellow, making you wonder if it should be classed as a gold centre. It was seen on the show bench in 1950, and it seems to have retained its vigour, offsetting quite readily. Raised by James Douglas in 1931. (See photo on page 85.)

'Polestar'

A variety in purple shades, raised by Derek Telford.

'Rabley Heath'

A desirable plant, bred by Allan Hawkes in 1972 and named after the area where he lives, in Hertfordshire, England. The flowers are bright, purple-blue shaded to pale blue. It is reasonably vigorous, offsetting quite freely. Exhibited in 1982.

'Rameses'

A purple shaded Alpine. This variety was raised by Derek Telford in 1992.

'Rose Kaye'

Beautiful flowers, strongly shaded from rich crimson to light pink. Les always said he would name his best plant after his wife and this is it. This variety takes considerable skill to achieve a winning plant, but it will reward any grower with a beautiful head of strongly shaded pips. 'Rose Kaye' was awarded Best Alpine Seedling at Cheadle in 1986.

'Rowena'

This old and popular variety regularly shows well. It is an excellent plant with strongly shaded purple-mauve blooms, and has won prizes for many years. Raised by Jack Stant of Huddersfield, England.

'Rowena'

'Roxburgh'

'Sandra'

'Stonnal'

'Roxburgh'

Lightly shaded, deep violet to violet-mauve blooms with an almost true-white centre. This is an old Douglas variety from before 1915.

'Sandra'

The pips of 'Sandra' are in shades of mauve with a small, well-defined centre. It was raised by Hal Cohen in 1973 and shown in 1974. It is an exquisite plant when grown well.

'Stonnal'

An attractive Alpine raised by Arthur Delbridge in 1978 with pips in rich purple shaded to delicate light mauve. 'Stonnal' was named after the area where Arthur Delbridge lives.

'Ted Gibbs'

'Thetis'

'Summer Sky'

A vigorous, attractive plant, shaded mid- to pale sky-blue, with a small, clearly defined centre. Raised by James Douglas prior to 1936.

'Susan'

Light blue shades. Of unknown origin.

'Symphony'

Light purple-blue shaded to dark purple, with an almost white centre. Raised by Arthur Delbridge. My plant flowered with only five petals, but it could be our growing methods.

'Ted Gibbs'

A lovely plant, the petals are strongly shaded crimson to a pale pinkish mauve. Raised from a 'C. W. Needham' and 'Vee Too' cross, by Ken Bowser of York, England, in 1986.

'Thetis'

A classic plant that has stood the test of time and still regularly appears on the show bench. Some authorities maintain that it was bred by G. Douglas around 1947, but an old handwritten list of Gordon

Douglas' mentions it as being first listed in James Douglas' catalogue in 1906. It is a striking plant with dark blue shaded to mid-blue petals. 'Thetis' can be temperamental, but it is well worth continued effort.

'Valerie'

The pips are dark mauve shaded to light mauve. An excellent variety for the show bench. Raised by Allan Hawkes, in 1969, from an unnamed seedling crossed with 'Paragon'. Shown in 1971. 'Valerie' is an easy, free-flowering plant.

'Vee Too'

The sister plant to 'Valerie' (see above), bred by Allan Hawkes. The flowers are crimson shaded to light wine; it could be likened to a darker 'Phyllis Douglas'. It was shown in 1980.

'Victoria de Wemyss'

Raised by Jack Wemyss-Cooke in 1979 from a batch of unflowered seedlings given to him by Derek Telford. A beautiful, very popular plant, strongly shaded deep to light blue, which performs well on the show bench. Exhibited in 1981.

'Valerie'

'Vulcan'

'Vulcan'

Frank Faulkner raised this vigorous and easy plant in 1955, from a 'Joy' and 'Peggy' cross. The flat pips are shaded purple to light pinkish purple, with a narrow edge. Shown in the 1960s.

'Walton'

'Walton' is a classic and much sought-after plant that was raised by Gordon Douglas in 1957. It is also known as 'Lavender Lady'. A symphony in bluish violet shades.

'Y. I. Hinney'

A lovely and distinct variety raised by Derek Telford in 1990. The petals are dark maroon-crimson shading to a narrow edge of pale creamy pink. The name is a Geordie expression that can be roughly translated as 'Hello dear'.

BORDERS

THESE PLANTS are for the garden. The named plants in cultivation have either been found growing in a garden (these are often very old varieties) or have been specifically bred for their strength, vigour and beauty, in that order.

As previously discussed, they require a good, humus-rich soil and shade, but given these conditions, they are easy and rewarding plants for any garden. Many enthusiasts like to grow them in pots and, given the same treatment as other pot-grown auriculas, they will delight you in spring with their large, fragrant heads of flowers.

ORIGINS

Border auriculas have been grown in British gardens for hundreds of years, and many of the names are purely descriptive, for example 'Old Irish Blue'. It is possible that some varieties were originally bred by Florists but, as they did not achieve the standards required for showing, were planted in the garden. Only the most vigorous would survive this treatment for many years, and thus the old varieties still available, having survived this long, are eminently suitable for the garden.

Although the Border auriculas have been recognized and grown for hundreds of years, it is only in the last 50 years that a few new varieties have been specifically bred for the garden. The work of Geoffrey Nicolle, in collecting and maintaining the Border auricula, has done much to conserve and rescue old varieties that would otherwise be lost. Bill and Simon Lockyer have bred several new varieties specifically for the garden; their nursery is one of the very few with a reasonable list of Border auriculas.

At present there is a lot of interest in the Border auriculas and many other growers are concentrating their efforts in producing good new varieties of sufficient strength and vigour. These new varieties are appearing in increasing numbers at the shows. In the last 10–15 years

'Old Yellow Dusty Miller'

RECOMMENDED VARIETIES

'Blue Velvet'

'Broadwell Gold'

'Dales Red'

'Lockyer's Supreme'

'Old Yellow Dusty Miller'

'Paradise Yellow'

'Dales Red'

the range of Borders available has increased dramatically, and they are achieving wider recognition as a good garden plant.

As gardeners are becoming more aware of the beauty and ease of cultivation of the Border auriculas, due both to displays at spring flower shows and exposure in the gardening press, their interest in them and desire to grow them is also increasing.

DESCRIPTION

There are no strict standards for the Border auriculas. Some have similarities to the Show auriculas while many others are like the Alpines. A good Border auricula will be a strong, healthy plant, with a good head of attractive flowers held well above the foliage on a sturdy stem. The flowers should not be ruined by rain, and the plant should be of sufficient vigour to over-winter and flower well in the garden.

The variety 'Dusty Miller' is fairly close to the wild *Primula auricula*; 'Dusty Miller' has come to be used as a broad descriptive term covering any auriculas with heavily mealed foliage, hence there are several different varieties of 'Old Yellow Dusty Miller', all equally entitled to the name.

There is considerable overlap between *Primula* x *pubescens* varieties and Border auriculas, which is not surprising considering they share the same ancestry.

'Aubergine'

A Border of unknown origin with aubergine coloured flowers.

'Belgravia Gold'

A variety that has golden-yellow, flat flowers, with no frills.

'Bellamy Pride'

Brian Walker bred this lovely variety around 1990. The large, flat flowers open white shading to pink, but they tend to age.

'Blue Mist'

A very old variety, with clear blue, medium-sized pips that are slightly ruffled.

'Blue Velvet'

A strong plant with rich dark blue, fragrant, thrum-eyed flowers with a distinct white eye. The leaves are bright green, with serrated edges, and are devoid of meal. 'Blue Velvet' is sweetly scented.

'Bradmore Bluebell'

Gwen Baker bred this light blue, thrum-eyed Border, which is rather small and not a good grower. It should possibly be classed as a *Primula* x *pubescens* rather than a Border, as its small size is nearer to the original species.

'Bramley Rose'

Rose-red, very frilly flowers make this plant, bred by Ike Hawthorn, particularly distinctive.

'Broadwell Gold'

A spectacular plant that was found by Joe Elliott in a garden in Gloucestershire, in 1950. It has large heads of thrum-eyed, bright yellow flowers with a prominent white eye and heavily mealed leaves. It was exhibited in 1952. There are impostors in circulation masquerading under this name. (See photo on page 28.)

'Bucks Green'

This has similarities to a Show green, but is a tough, easy plant for the garden.

'Chamois'

John Mercer raised this lovely and distinct variety, which produces huge heads of slightly frilled, pin-eyed flowers, the colour of a clean chamois leather. A cross between *P.* x *pubescens* 'Rufus' and a yellow Border auricula.

'Cooper's Gold'

Chris Gayfer discovered this plain gold Border growing in a Kingston-upon-Thames garden. It always presents a very fresh appearance.

'Craig Dhu'

A very dark red Border with a yellow tube and mealed leaves. It was introduced by Mr. A. Duguid of Edrom Nursery in Scotland.

'Curry Blend'

Ike Hawthorn raised this variety, which has curry-yellow flowers with a cream centre.

'Dales Red'

An attractive plant with rich red flowers shading to almost black, contrasting with the pale, lightly farinated centre. 'Dales Red' is a vigorous plant that is easy to grow.

'Dick Rodgers'

A browny gold Border with a light centre.

'Doctor Lennon's White'

This old Border, which has white flowers, is now a very scarce variety.

'Dusky Yellow'

Unfortunately the flower stem is too weak to support the dull yellow flowers.

'Blue Velvet'

'Chamois'

'Dales Red'

'George Swinford's Leathercoat'

'Emma Elizabeth'

A very popular plant with big blowsy flowers of pinky mauve shading to dark mauve, with a large, white, scalloped centre. It is highly scented.

'Frittenden Yellow'

A yellow Border whose flower stems are often too thin to support the flower head in poor weather.

'George Swinford's Leathercoat'

An old variety discovered at Filkins, Oxfordshire, England, by Ruth Duthie, this is commonly known as 'Leathercoat'. It has pale beige-pink flowers and serrated, well-mealed foliage. Many plants in circulation as 'Old Pink Dusty Miller' are in fact 'George Swinford's Leathercoat'. While this variety is reputed to be feeble, we have sold it in recent years and have not found this to be so.

'Jezebel'

A lovely variety with very frilly maroon flowers which contrast with the light eye. 'Jezebel' has very little scent.

'Kristen Stripe'

As the name suggests, this Border, in maroon shades, is a striped variety. Because it has floppy footstalks, the flowers tend to hang.

'Lambert's Gold'

A golden, unscented Border.

'Lavender Lady'

This variety, one of the new Border auriculas, was grown by Steve and Marlene Craven of North Yorkshire, England, from Border seed. It has attractive lavender flowers with a white eye.

'Lemon Sherbet'

A Border with large lemon flowers.

'Linnet'

An old and dainty Border, with fawn, primrose and brown flowers.

'Lintz'

A good Border with flowers of velvety brown. This variety has won awards at the Southern Section shows. Discovered by Lawrence Wigley in a nurseryman's frame.

'Lockyer's Charm'

A poor grower with blue flowers and a farinated, white eye. It was raised by Bill and Simon Lockyer of Purley, in London.

'Lockyer's Frilly'

This variety has mauve shaded to dark maroon-purple flowers, with a lightly farinated white eye and farinated leaves. 'Lockyer's Frilly' was raised by

'Lavender Lady'

Bill and Simon Lockyer in 1996 from a 'Royal Velvet' and 'Purple Velvet' cross.

'Lockyer's Gem'

Very distinct, large flowers – purple, slashed and striped unevenly with yellow. There is no farina on the leaves or flowers. It was raised by Bill and Simon Lockyer in 1989, the result of a cross between an unnamed violet Border and 'Paradise Yellow'.

'Lockyer's Green'

A typical, green-edged Border, tough and easy to grow. It was raised by Bill and Simon Lockyer, from a 'Bucks Green' and 'Osbourne Green' cross.

'Lockyer's Supreme'

This highly scented variety with apricot flowers was raised by the Lockyers from a 'Bellamy Pride' and 'Old Irish Blue' cross.

'McWatt's Blue'

This is a lovely old variety, raised by Dr McWatt. It has rich, purple-blue flowers with a large, well-farinated white eye and densely mealed leaves.

'Lockyer's Frilly'

'Lockyer's Gem'

'McWatt's Blue'

'Old Clove Red'

'Misty'

This is a shaded, grey-blue Border. Bred by Anne Rowe in 1998.

'Mrs A. Harrison'

One of the better Border yellows, highly scented, with good-sized flowers, a ring of paste, and lightly mealed leaves.

'Mrs Cairn's Old Blue'

This variety is an example of a thrum-eyed plant. It has flowers of light blue shading to violet, with a cream centre.

'Mrs Harris'

'Mrs Harris' is a pin-eyed plant with big, blowsy, pale yellow flowers.

'Old Clove Red'

This variety is probably descended from the Show selfs. The smallish flowers are a rich dark red, with a mealed centre. (See photo on page 95.)

'Old Gold Dusty Miller'

Mary McMurtrie introduced this rare plant with highly mealed foliage.

'Old Irish Blue'

A lovely, delicate plant that cannot be too highly recommended. The flowers are shaded dark to light blue, scented and frilly. There are plants available under this name that are not the true plant – the true plant has a long, thin carrot and plain, unmealed leaves. 'Old Irish Blue' was shown at the Chelsea Flower Show in the 1920s.

'Old Irish Scented'

This variety was raised in Co. Sligo, Ireland. It has dull yellow, thrum-eyed flowers, which are pleasantly scented.

'Old Mustard'

A nondescript plant with mustard yellow flowers.

'Old Pink Dusty Miller'

This variety has pink flowers and mealed leaves.

'Old Purple Dusty Miller'

As the name suggests, this variety has small purple flowers and mealed leaves.

'Old Red Dusty Miller'

This is the best-known 'Dusty Miller', apart from the yellow, but unfortunately, many of the plants that are available under this name are not true. In fact, the little *Auricula* x *pubescens* 'Gnome' is sometimes christened 'Old Red Dusty Miller'. The true plant has small, dark ox-blood red flowers that do not open flat, and the heavily mealed leaves of a true 'Dusty Miller'.

'Old Suffolk Bronze'

A lovely old Border with plain red, frilled flowers, edged with ginger.

'Old Tawny'

This variety is a relatively small plant, with brown, pin-eyed flowers.

'Old White Dusty Miller'

'Old White Dusty Miller' is a very rare plant. As the name suggests, it has white flowers and the typical, thickly mealed leaves of a Dusty Miller.

'Old Yellow Dusty Miller'

'Old Yellow Dusty Miller' is very close to the wild yellow *Primula auricula*. It has sweetly scented yellow flowers and heavily mealed leaves. (See photo on page 90.)

'Osbourne Green'

This variety is a vigorous plant. The flowers are purple-and-green with very ragged edges to the petals and a huge cream centre. An old, green-edged Border, it was found in 1983, in an old cottage garden in Ireland, and was named after the owner of the cottage, Mr Osbourne.

'Paradise Yellow'

'Paradise Yellow' is one of the loveliest Border auriculas around. This plant has good heads of bright yellow flowers, which often form a completely round head of colour, similar to a drumstick primula. It was found in the Mediterranean in 1960, by Sir Cedric Morris, and named after the nursery that introduced it, Paradise Nursery, in Suffolk, England. 'Paradise Yellow' is a vigorous and easy plant.

'Purple Velvet'

'Purple Velvet' is one of the best of the old Border auriculas. It is a lovely plant with deep, velvety purple, slightly ruffled flowers which are held on strong, sturdy stems.

'Old Irish Blue'

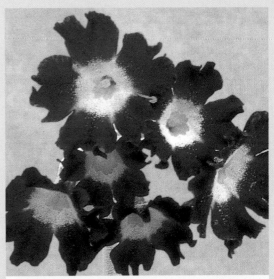

'Old Red Dusty Miller'

'Osbourne Green'

'Queen Alexandra'

'Queen Alexandra'

An old Irish variety with heads of large, pale biscuit-yellow flowers with a beautiful scent. If pot-grown for showing, keep it well shaded as it fades easily.

'Robbo'

A lovely new Border, of unknown origin, that has gingery brown flowers.

'Royal Velvet'

A vigorous plant with large, bright crimson-purple flowers with frilled petals and a large cream eye.

'Ruby Hyde'

Cherry red flowers with a creamy yellow centre make this a distinct and eye-catching variety. Introduced by Bob Bach.

'Southport'

'Starling'

'Truman'

'Winifred'

'Sarah Suzanne'

A beautifully scented plant with deep blue, white-eyed flowers, and lightly mealed leaves.

'Silas'

A good modern Border raised by Steve and Marlene Craven in 1995. It has shaded gold, slightly ruffled petals and a bright pale eye.

'Snow White'

A small plant with clear white flowers.

'Southport'

Small, vivid brick red flowers with a yellow eye and light, bright green leaves with no farina. Once rare, this old variety is becoming more readily available, but lacks the vigour of many other Borders.

'Saint Gerrans' White'

An old Border that has creamy white flowers with a yellow eye, and no farina on the leaves.

'Starling'

Now for something completely different. The colour is best described as very dark slate purple, lightly powdered with farina. The small flowers can form a completely round head. Raised by Chris Gayfer.

'Tawny Owl'

Attractive, tawny brown flowers without scent.

'Truman'

A vigorous and easy plant with frilly flowers of red, brown and beige and a rich gold centre.

'Windways Mystery'

The late Bernard Smith raised this scented Border auricula. It has medium-sized, pin-eyed flowers of mustard brown, with a white eye.

'Winifred'

Not to be confused with the gold-centred Alpine auricula 'Winnifrid' (see description on page 75), this plant has frilly flowers of gold, brown and yellow. 'Winifred' is a vigorous and easy Border, ideal for the garden.

'Winward Blue'

This Border produces large heads of sky blue flowers with a white eye.

DOUBLES

SOME OF THE Double auriculas can be grown in the garden, and the fully double flowers are very attractive and often sweetly scented. However, they do need ideal conditions, and most of the modern varieties listed have been bred for the beauty of the flower rather than for garden vigour, and are therefore more suitable for pot culture. The current range of Doubles is derived from crosses between Alpine, Border and Show auriculas.

There has been an explosion of new Doubles being raised in the last 10 years, and some of the varieties described here are not yet in general circulation. I have tried to select those that I think are most likely to become available commercially, or that will be of significance to hybridizers in the future.

ORIGINS

Although the Double auriculas were widely grown in the past, for many years they were neglected, being classed as not worthy of the attention of the Florists in Britain. However, in the USA, Ralph Balcom of Seattle and Denna Snuffer of Oregon bred new strains of these lovely plants successfully for many years, mainly from Border auriculas, and their work led to a re-awakening of interest both in the USA and in Britain. Many of the Doubles in cultivation today can trace their ancestry back to Balcom and Snuffer seed.

Jared Sinclair, of Barnhaven in Cumbria, developed strains of Double auricula seed based on the North American Doubles, and several of the varieties grown today were raised from his seed.

RECOMMENDED VARIETIES

'Albert Bailey'
'Doublure'
'Doyen'
'Little Rosetta'
'Mary'
'Matthew Yates'   'Doyen'

Ken Gould was given some American Doubles in 1958, and from them, in 1961, he raised 'Mary' and 'Catherine'. These plants played an important role in the raising of Doubles in subsequent years.

During the 1970s and 1980s there was a gradual increase in the numbers of exhibitors, including growers such as Allan Hawkes, Ron Cole and Len Bailey, and new plants, but it was not until the end of the 1980s, and into the next decade, that the popularity of the Doubles dramatically increased.

In 1976, a class for three plants was added to the previous single- and two-plant classes at the Northern Auricula Show – a reflection of the increasing popularity of the Doubles. Over the next few years, the work of Gwen Baker had a profound effect on the development of the modern Doubles; her plants and articles have inspired many of the Doubles hybridizers of the 1990s.

During the 1990s many new auriculas were bred by Derek Salt, Ken Whorton, Laura Pickin, Len Bailey and Keith Leeming, to name but a few, and the Double became a recognized auricula for showing, not just

A collection of the Double auriculas bred by Derek Salt. Left to right, from top: 'Terror-cotta', 'May', 'Joanne', 'Sue Ritchie', 'Brenda Hyatt', 'Fred Booley', 'Aquarius' and 'Magic'

another type with no clear standards. In 1990 the Northern Section of the National Auricula and Primula Society endorsed proposals drawn up by Alan Guest. These were, in fact, an extension of those already used by the Midland and West, and Southern Sections.

Since then the Northern Section has re-defined the show standards for Doubles in order to bring them closer to the basic standards of the Florists' auricula. (These new standards are included in their entirety in Appendix 1, on page 169.)

Their purpose is to give modern breeders the scope to develop differing types of petal conformation (resembling, for example, camellias, begonias, carnations, dahlias, roses etc), and also flaked and striped petals, but always so that they are consistent with the characteristics of the Florists' auricula (ie regarding the circularity of pip, rounded, unnotched petals and symmetry).

DESCRIPTION

Although the Doubles are not officially grouped in this way, the following divisions have been adopted for the sake of ease in describing them: classical, standard and informal. In classical Doubles the petals are laid over each other in a regular manner, as in a camellia. Standard Doubles have more petals, and the formation is irregular, as in an old-fashioned double rose. The lay of the petals in informal Doubles is neither regular nor symmetrical.

'Albert Bailey'

Len Bailey raised this delicate, pale orange Double in 1988, from a 'Jane Myers' and 'Walton Heath' cross, and named it after his brother.

'Albury'

This vigorous, dark red to purple variety is similar to 'Shalford' (see description on page 112) and was raised by W. R. Hecker in the late 1960s.

'Ann Hyatt'

An attractive Double of classical form, in apricot-yellow shades. Raised by Matthew Rouane in 1992.

'Aztec'

This lime-gold Double of informal form has been a prizewinner at Midland and West, and Northern shows. It was bred by Ken Whorton, in 1997, from a 'Hoghton Gem' and 'Frank Bailey' cross.

'Bacchante'

This variety has flowers of a lovely dark wine, with tightly folded petals. It was bred by Ken Whorton in 1998 from a red seedling and 'Susannah' cross, and has won prizes at the Midland and West, and Northern shows.

'Bella'

A light pink Double, bred by Ken Whorton, in 1997, from a 'Calypso' and 'Helena Dean' cross.

'Blakeney'

A purple Double of unknown origin, and not really distinct from many other purple Doubles.

'Brownie'

Rosetta Jones raised this striking North American russet-brown Double.

'Calypso'

A marmalade-orange, classical Double, bred by Ken Whorton in 1990; another prizewinner at the Midland and West, and Northern Shows. It came from a (pink Double x 'Westcott Pride') and 'Hoghton Gem' cross.

'Camelot'

A vigorous and easy variety with heavy heads of purple flowers, raised by Ken Gould in 1967, from a 'Nigel' and 'Watt's Purple' cross. It was exhibited in 1968. The flowers of 'Camelot' tend to hang, as they are too heavy for the footstalks.

'Cameo Beauty'

A truly beautiful Double with folded petals in cream and yellow. Bred by Ken Whorton from a ('Bilton' x 'Mary' x 'Hoghton Gem') and 'Susannah' cross and first shown in 1994. It received an Award of Merit and Best Plant in Show award at the 1995 Midland Show. Gwen Baker said it was the finest Double she had ever seen. Let us hope that it will become generally available.

'Catherine'

This variety, a slightly frilled classical Double, has flowers of a lovely lemon yellow with a hint of lime green. It was bred by Ken Gould in 1961, from seed sent by Ralph Balcom, from Seattle, USA. (See photo on page 104.)

'Chantilly Cream'

A vigorous plant with pale yellow flowers, fuller than those of 'Diamond'. Raised by Gwen Baker in 1980. (See photo on page 104.)

'Chiquita'

A fully imbricate Double of rich ginger shades. Bred by Ken Whorton from a 'Digit' and 'Susannah' cross, and introduced in 1997. It was given an Award of Merit at the Midland Show in 1997.

'Chocolate Mousse'

Not surprisingly, 'Chocolate Mousse' is a rich chocolate brown. Raised by Keith Leeming.

'Bacchante'

'Bella'

'Camelot'

'Cameo Beauty'

'Cinnamon'

An attractive ginger Double. Raised by Keith Leeming, in 1989, from an unflowered seedling – a 'Jane Myers' and 'Walton Heath' cross – given to him by Len Bailey. (See photo on page 105.)

'Corrie Files'

This attractive variety is a red Double of classical form. 'Corrie Files' was raised by Cliff Timpson, in 1990, from 'Sirius' seed.

'Crimson Glow'

A lovely red Double, bred by Ken Whorton in 1998 – the result of **line breeding**, involving 'Winnifrid', the crimson Alpine. A brighter red than 'Doyen', it offsets very readily. (See photo on page 105.)

'Catherine'

'Chantilly Cream'

'Daydream'

A creamy white, classical Double that has won prizes at the Midland and West, and Northern shows. Bred by Ken Whorton, in 1996, from a 'Jungfrau' and 'Hoghton Gem' cross.

'Delilah'

A vigorous, deep, dark purple-red, raised by Gwen Baker in 1979. Unfortunately, it tends to age quickly.

'Denna Snuffer'

A pale, creamy yellow that was first introduced by Mr Smith, from the North American Doubles, in 1964. It tends to be open-centred, which can make it unsuitable for the show bench.

'Devon Cream'

Huge, creamy yellow flowers. Easy and vigorous.

'Diamond'

A pale, creamy white that can be semi-double. Bred by Gwen Baker in 1977, from a ('Mary' x 'Gordon Douglas') and 'Catherine' cross.

'Digby'

Dark purple and fully double. Raised by Derek Salt, in 1990, from an 'Albury' and 'Shalford' cross.

'Digit'

A lovely gold Double of classical form, bred by Ken Whorton and first shown in 1992.

'Doublet'

'Doublet' is an easy, reliable, purple Double that makes a good garden plant. It was raised by Allan Hawkes in 1975.

'Doublure'

Fully double, imbricate flowers of a dark reddish purple. Bred from a 'Susannah' and 'Walton Heath' cross, it was raised by Allan Hawkes in 1980. (See photo on page 106.)

'Doyen'

Gwen Baker raised this vigorous and easy variety in 1982. It has rich, dark mahogany-crimson flowers of classical form. (See photo on page 106.)

'Cinnamon'

'Crimson Glow'

'Delilah'

'Denna Snuffer'

'Dusty Double'

'Dusty Double', an old-fashioned Double grown in the USA, was raised by Cy Happy in the 1950s. The flowers, described as lavender green, are striped with silver and lightly coated with meal. While this is a very hardy plant that offsets freely, the flowers do need protection if you wish to enjoy the full beauty of the meal.

'Dusty Lemon'

A yellow Double raised by B. Smith, from seed supplied by Cy Happy.

'Emberglow'

A bright orange-red, full, frilly Double, raised by Martin Sheader in 1990.

'Doublure'

'Doyen'

'Emily'

A new North American Double raised by Dan Pederson of Tacoma. It is described as creamy white infused with green, yellow and pink.

'Fantasia'

A seedling, bred by Ken Whorton in 1999, that attempts to widen the range of Double auriculas, as encouraged by the revised Standards of the Northern Society, by introducing flaking and striping. 'Fantasia' is a good example of the new breed of auriculas, of which we hope to see more in the future.

'Firsby'

A cream Double, raised by Derek Salt.

'Fishtoft'

A lilac Double of standard form. 'Fishtoft' was raised by Derek Salt, in 1980, from an 'Oaklea Rose' and 'Walton Heath' cross.

'Frank Bailey'

This variety is a very full, gold Double. Raised by Len Bailey in the early 1990s, from a 'Jane Myers' and 'Walton Heath' cross.

'Fred Booley'

A dark blue classical Double, introduced by Derek Salt in 1999, in which year it won the Premier Seedling award at Datchet. Bred from a 'Quatro' and 'Sarah Lodge' cross.

'Funny Valentine'

A very good dark red from Eddy Pickin, bred from a 'Helena Dean' and 'Doyen' cross.

'Gaia'

'Gaia' is a vigorous plant with buff flowers that are fully double. It was raised by Martin Sheader in 1974, from Barnhaven seed.

'Gold Seal'

A gold-flushed orange Double of classical form, which won the Premier and Best in Show awards at Knowle in 1998, and the Premier award at Cheadle, also in 1998. Bred by Ken Whorton, in 1996, from a 'Digit' and 'Helena Dean' cross.

'Fantasia'

'Fred Booley'

'Gold Seal'

'Golden Hind'

'Golden Chartreuse'

A lovely, vigorous, golden-yellow Double, though of poor form. Raised by Gwen Black in 1980, from Barnhaven seed.

'Golden Hind'

Another glorious Double from Ken Whorton, who bred this striking gold-and-brown bicolour in 1993.

Unfortunately, because it is slow to produce offsets, it is not yet widely distributed.

'Golden Splendour'

A glorious shade of old gold and a lovely form, this is a vigorous plant with plenty of offsets. Raised by Keith Leeming, in 1987, from an unflowered seedling given to him by Len Bailey. It comes from a 'Jane Myers' and 'Walton Heath' cross.

'Grand Slam'

This blood orange Double of informal form has been a prizewinner at both the Midland and West, and Northern shows. Bred by Ken Whorton, in 1998, from a 'Sir Robert' and 'Frank Bailey' cross.

'Guinea Gold'

Hal Cohen raised this golden-yellow Double in 1979, from Barnhaven seed.

'Gwen Baker'

A beautiful, pale yellow, classical Double. Raised by Derek Salt, in 1988, from a Barnhaven F2 and 'Diamond' cross, and named in honour of Gwen Baker, Queen of the Doubles, who has done so much work in the breeding of new varieties.

'Grand Slam'

'Helena Dean'

'Helena Dean' is a pale yellow Double of classical form. It was raised by Len Bailey, in 1977, from a 'Jane Myers' and 'Sarah Lodge'cross and has since proved to be an excellent parent in the breeding of new varieties.

'Hoghton Gem'

A golden-yellow of standard form which has been used extensively as a parent. It was raised by D. Cornforth, in 1976, from Barnhaven seed.

'Jane Myers No. 1'

This variety is a primrose-yellow Double. It was bred by Len Bailey, in 1976, from a Barnhaven semi-double and 'Mary' cross.

'Jane Myers No. 2'

A similar Double to the preceding plant but more vigorous. Raised by Len Bailey in 1978 from a 'Jane Myers No. 1' and 'Sarah Lodge' cross.

'Jungfrau'

A late-flowering variety with large cream flowers of a lovely shape. Raised by Les Wright in 1980.

'Kentucky Blues'

A breakthrough in blue Doubles, 'Kentucky Blues' was bred by Randall Dee in 1999. Hopefully it will become readily available.

'Kirklands'

A purple with full wavy petals, of unknown origin.

'Lima'

This variety is a lime-yellow Double of classical form. It was bred by Ken Whorton, in 1989, from a 'Hoghton Gem' and 'Mary' cross. Among other prizes, it was the recipient of the Premier award at Saltford in 1993.

'Lincoln Imp'

A buff Double with a raspberry centre. 'Lincoln Imp' was raised by Derek Salt, in 1996, from his own Doubles seed.

'Little Rosetta'

A fully double plant with large, reddish brown flowers. Raised by B. Smith in 1980. 'Little Rosetta' is vigorous and easy.

'Gwen Baker'

'Lincoln Imp'

'Little Rosetta'

'Marigold'

'Maid Marion'

Ken Gould raised this pale, primrose-yellow Double in 1963, from seed off 'Mary'.

'Marigold'

This plant has incredibly frilled, fully double flowers of an unusual dark marigold orange. It needs careful dressing and thinning to show well. Raised by Dr Robert Newton, in 1964, from an F2 Meeks Double and 'Minstead' cross. 'Marigold' is a plant that inspires either love or hate.

'Marigold Sports'

This is the name we gave to a batch of micropropagated 'Marigold' that we bought in 1987 which produced leaves and flowers with identical form to the true 'Marigold' flowers, but in shades ranging from brown and orange right through to very pale yellow.

'Mary'

One of my favourites, and not just because of the name. It has pale yellow flowers of a lovely shape. Introduced by Ken Gould, around 1960, from seed from Ralph Balcom of Seattle, USA. It is the sister to 'Catherine' (see description on page 102). 'Mary' has proved to be a good seed parent.

'Matthew Yates'

A particularly distinctive Double with very, very dark purple, almost black flowers, which are very double. Len Bailey raised this variety in 1980 from a 'Jane Myers' and 'Walton Heath' cross. A good plant for the show bench.

'May Morning'

An apricot-pink Double of informal form. Bred by Ken Whorton in 1993 from a (pink Double x 'Westcott Pride') and 'Hoghton Gem' cross, that has been a prizewinner at the Midland and West, and Northern shows.

'Mermaid'

This variety, with small, red flowers, is of unknown origin. It has a tendency to go single when it receives insufficient food.

'Mipsie Miranda'

The flowers of this variety are light yellow and of good form. It was raised by Hazel Wood, in 1982, from Barnhaven seed. Thought to have been lost, it reappeared and started producing offsets.

'Mish Mish'

A peach to buff variety that has two rows of petals. It was raised by B. Smith, from Cy Happy seed.

'Moonstone'

A lemon-yellow, classical Double. Raised by Gwen

Baker in 1980 and shown in 1981. It is an easy variety that offsets well.

'Mrs Dargan'

A very old variety that was found in an Irish garden. Believed to be of eighteenth-century origin. It has yellow petals, faintly striped with red. Nowadays, it is usually only semi-double.

'Nigel'

Ken Gould raised this violet, almost black, Double in 1962, from Balcom seed. Reputedly hard to keep in good health.

'Nita'

An attractive, near-white, fully double variety. Derek Salt raised 'Nita', in 1994, from Donnington Plants' Double seed.

'Nymph'

This caramel-cream, very full Double has been a prizewinner at the Midland and West, and Northern shows. Bred by Ken Whorton, in 1995, from the same cross as 'Cameo Beauty'.

'Old Double Green'

An interesting plant that was discovered in Ireland. The fully double flower of 'Old Double Green' is covered with meal, as is the foliage.

'Paphos'

A lovely wine purple of very good form. Raised by Keith Leeming and shown in 1998. It has won several prizes.

'Pink Fondant'

A good and vigorous, light mauve-pink Double of standard form. Raised by Tim Coop in 1979, from Barnhaven seed.

'Prometheus'

A fully double red, raised by Martin Sheader.

'Mary'

'Matthew Yates'

'Paphos'

'Pink Fondant'

'Rapp's Double Purple'

This popular North American plant has been widely grown in the Seattle/Tacoma area for 15 years or more. Raised by Al Rapp, it has rich purple flowers on sturdy stems, and offsets readily.

'Rosamund'

Martin Sheader raised this old rose Double.

'Sarah Brightman'

Described as pink on cream, this Double, of standard form, was raised by Dreena and Martin Thompson in 1991.

'Sarah Gisby'

A lovely Double that was given the Award of Merit at Knowle in 1997, and the Premier award at

Cheadle in the same year. The flowers are purplish brown with a lighter edge, and present a well-rounded outline. The form is exquisite. It was bred by Ken Whorton, in 1997, from a 'Golden Hind' and 'Doublet' cross, and named after his daughter. 'Sarah Gisby' offsets fairly readily.

'Sarah Lodge'

A lovely, light mauve-purple Double. Raised by Ron Cole, in 1974, from Barnhaven seed, and shown in 1975. Named after Ron Cole's mother.

'Shalford'

'Shalford', a reddish purple Double, was raised by W. Hecker in 1965.

'Sherbet'

A fully double lime-green variety. Raised by Derek Salt in 1997.

'Sibsey'

A bluish Double with an open centre. Raised by Derek Salt in 1989 from an 'Oaklea Rosebud' and 'Walton Heath' cross.

'Sir Robert'

This pink, open-centred Double was raised by Lester Smith, in 1959, from the North American Balcom Doubles. Named after Sir Robert Ewbank, who was popularly known as Sir Robert.

'Snowmaiden'

The first pure-white Double, raised by Randall Dee, in 1998, from a 'Sea Mist' and 'Helena Dean' cross. A plant to look for in the future.

'South Barrow'

A dark, reddish purple Double. Raised by Ken Gould in 1962, and shown in 1971.

'Standish'

A beige-cream Double, raised by Allan Guest, in

1970, from Barnhaven seed. Seen on the show bench in 1980.

'Stripey'

Derek Salt raised this interesting plant in 1984, from Barnhaven seed. The small flowers are described as yellow-streaked purple.

'Sun Maiden'

Another beautiful Double, bred by Ken Whorton in 1996. This has won prizes at the Midland and West, and Northern shows. A rich gold of classical form, it came from a 'Digit' and 'Helena Dean' cross.

'Susannah'

This popular and widely grown plant has attractive and very double flowers; the doubling is in four quarters, like an old-fashioned rose. Raised by Allan Hawkes in the 1960s.

'Sword'

A green-edged Double, of curiosity value more than anything. Raised by Derek Salt from a 'Fleminghouse' and 'Prague' cross.

'Terror-cotta'

This variety has flowers of brick red, as indicated by the name. Raised by Derek Salt from a yellow seedling and 'Mary' cross. It was a prizewinner at Datchet in 1999.

'The Cardinal'

This variety is said to have originated in the garden of Cardinal Richelieu in France. It has flowers of a deep, blood-red crimson.

'Thirlmere'

A purple shaded classical Double, raised by Gwen Baker in 1984.

'Trouble'

Derek Salt raised this classical Double in 1988. The

'Sarah Gisby'

'Sarah Lodge'

'Susannah'

'Terror-cotta'

flowers are a strange beige-coffee colour. 'Trouble' displays near-perfect form and is a regular prizewinner. (See photo on page 114.)

'Walton Heath'

A light purple Double of classical form. Raised by Ken Gould in 1979 and seen on the show bench in 1985. Used extensively in hybridization.

'Watt's Purple'

A purple Double, raised by Watts of Denbigh, North Wales, that has proved to be good for breeding.

'Westcott Pride'

Dark and of standard form, shaded red to mauve. Raised by Ken Gould in 1967, from a 'Nigel' and 'Basuto' cross. A good parent plant. Offsets freely.

'Trouble'

'Winkle'

A 'Mary' seedling with small white flowers, raised by Ken Gould in 1964.

'Wrangle'

A bluish Double raised by Derek Salt, in 1992, from an 'Oaklea Rose' and 'Walton Heath' cross.

'Zambia'

An old variety with very dark red flowers. Raised by Ken Gould, in 1965, from a 'Nigel' and 'Watt's Purple' cross. It was shown in 1967.

SHOWS

The Show auriculas are divided into four sections: edges, selfs, fancies and stripes. All of these have a ring of glistening white paste around a rich yellow tube.

THE CLASSIFICATION OF SHOW AURICULAS

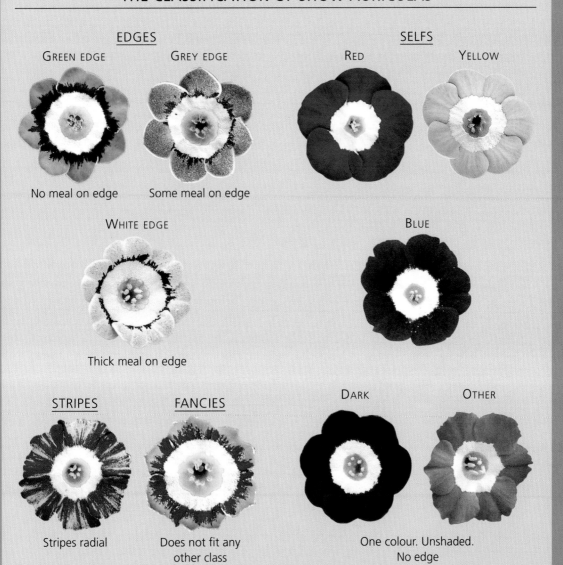

EDGES

GREEN EDGE — No meal on edge

GREY EDGE — Some meal on edge

WHITE EDGE — Thick meal on edge

SELFS

RED

YELLOW

BLUE

DARK — One colour. Unshaded. No edge

OTHER — One colour. Unshaded. No edge

STRIPES

Stripes radial

FANCIES

Does not fit any other class

EDGES

THE EDGES could be described as the aristocrats of the auricula world: they are the most challenging type to grow well.

ORIGINS

The edged auricula was born around 1740; a mutation occurred whereby the petal edges became leaf. Depending on the amount of meal, this could be green, grey or white. Soon after this, due to the hybridizers' work, many edges became available. As rain spoilt their paste and meal, these were grown under cover.

Until the end of the nineteenth century it was acceptable for edged auriculas to have a coloured **body colour**, including red, purple, rose, brown and violet. The compulsory black body colour seems to have been started by the Florists of Middleton, in Lancashire, England, in the late 1800s, and this standard was soon accepted by all. After this, any edge that did not comply was termed a fancy. The introduction of yellow into the range of body colours appears to be a twentieth-century development; in the early days, yellow was not acceptable for either edges or selfs.

DESCRIPTION

The edges are subdivided according to the colour of their edge. This is the outer part of the petal, and has the characteristics and colour of the leaf. Green-edged Shows are completely devoid of meal, with none on the flowers or the leaves, grey-edged Shows have a light sprinkling of meal on the edge and the leaves, and white-edged Shows have a heavy coating of meal on the edge and leaves. There is room for considerable overlap between the grey and white edges; many varieties can be in either class depending on cultivation.

China edge refers to a fault in green-edged auriculas in which there is a thin line of farina around the edges of the petals. Some exhibitors advocate separate classes for China edges, but purists regard this as a weakening of the standard.

The body colour should be black or very dark red, and smooth on the inside, feathering out into the edge. The colour or type of edge (ie green, grey or white) depends on the amount of meal that overlays it. The paste referred to is the white ring surrounding the yellow tube (the hole in the middle), which is covered in a thick layer of crystalline farina.

For too many years auricula breeders were tied down by convention; anything that did not conform to the old standards of black body and green, grey or white edge was felt to be inferior and was relegated to the ranks of the fancies. Times are changing. It is now acceptable for the body to be any colour, and as long as the edge is of sufficient quality, the plants will be judged alongside those with black bodies – a return to the original standards. We can now look forward to a riot of colour among the edges.

RECOMMENDED VARIETIES

Green edged
'Bob Lancashire'
'Prague'
'Fleminghouse'

Grey edged
'Lovebird'

White edged
'C. G. Haysom'
'James Arnot'

'Fleminghouse'

'Lovebird'

'James Arnot'

GREEN EDGED

'Beechen Green'

Raised by L. E. Wigley in 1970, who named it from a line in Keats' *Ode to a Nightingale*. It was shown in 1985. 'Beechen Green' is often lightly mealed, and has won a prize as a China edge.

'Bob Lancashire'

A reasonably good modern variety. Raised in 1984 by Jack Wemyss-Cooke by crossing 'Chloë' with 'Geldersome Green'. Exhibited in 1985.

'Chloë'

One of the finest greens, this variety was bred by F. Buckley, of Macclesfield, England, in 1957, and named after his wife. It was first shown in 1967. It boasts outstanding flower colour, and will produce six to seven blooms per truss. The broad, rounded, light green leaves are very distinct with their serrated margins. Reputedly, its vigour has deteriorated; certainly it has few offsets with us, but the plants are large and healthy.

'Chloris'

This variety was raised by F. Buckley in 1973. Said to be temperamental, it tends to break into small rosettes easily, and is difficult to flower. It was shown in 1983.

'Daphnis'

Another green edge raised by F. Buckley. It was shown in 1975.

'Doctor Duthie'

An interesting variety raised by Peter Ward, in 1975, from a 'Fleminghouse' and 'Chloë' cross. It has been awarded two Premiers, but is not thought of highly because it tends to have only three or four pips, and the petals do not always overlap properly, as can be seen from the photograph (opposite, bottom left). Cotton wool has been placed between the foot-stalks of the plant shown, before taking it to a show, to protect the flowers.

'Dorothy'

Raised by Jack Ballard in 1969 and shown in 1970.

'Emerald'

Raised by F. Buckley in 1962, and exhibited in 1972, this darker-than-usual green edge will sometimes perform well on the show bench. It is in very short supply, and rarely obtainable.

'Ettrick'

Another green edge raised by James Douglas.

'Figaro'

A lovely variety that shows great promise. 'Figaro' was raised by David Hadfield in 1985 from a 'Chloë' and 'Haffner' cross.

'Fleminghouse'

One of the best and a regular prizewinner at the shows. This fine variety was raised by Jack Stant in 1967, from seed provided by Dr Robert Newton. It is named after Fleminghouse Lane in Huddersfield, Yorkshire, England. This excellent variety has the flattest pips of all. Not only has it the breeding to be Best in Show, it is fairly easy to keep in good health and will give great pleasure to the grower, though it is often described as performing better in the north of England.

'Geldersome Green No. 2'

A reliable, reasonably vigorous variety that was bred by Jack Ballard, in 1970. It appeared on the show bench in 1971.

'Gleneagles'

'Gleneagles' was raised by Gordon Douglas in 1985 and shown in 1988.

'Glenluce'

Another green raised by Gordon Douglas, in 1985.

'Beechen Green'

'Bob Lancashire'

'Doctor Duthie'

'Fleminghouse'

'Green Jacket'

This variety is a challenge to grow, and very erratic in its flowering. It was raised by Jack Ballard and shown in 1970.

'Green Mouse'

A good, vigorous plant, but not good enough for showing. Raised by Stan Kos. It appeared on the show bench in 1970. The photo here shows a plant that would be much better if the pips had been thinned. (See photo on page 120.)

'Green Parrot'

Fairly easy, but not of show quality, so rarely seen on the show bench. It does, however, have a bright gold tube and dense paste. It was raised by James Douglas and shown in 1959.

'Green Mouse'

'Greenheart'

'Greenheart'

This sturdy and reliable plant was raised by Fred Buckley and shown in 1967. It is said that it could be losing its vigour, but we do not have any problems growing it.

'Greensleeves'

A strong grower that offsets rapidly. It was raised by Dr Robert Newton in 1958 and shown in 1959.

'Gretna Green'

A useful dark green; although not one of the most reliable, it can be very good. Raised by Fred Buckley.

'Gruener Veltliner'

A new green of great merit that was raised by Bob Taylor, in 1992, from an 'Orb' and 'Hew Dalrymple' cross. This variety shows great promise and is well worth seeking out.

'Haffner'

This 'Fleminghouse' seedling was raised by David Hadfield, in 1974, and was awarded the Corsar Cup in 1980. On its day it will produce large, darkish green, very flat blooms with a heavy body colour and a well-shaped tube: it can be very good. Good for breeding.

'Hew Dalrymple'

A strong grower of good habit with medium green flowers that can be very good. Raised by C. G. Haysom in 1947 and named after Haysom's employer and friend, Mr Dalrymple. It appeared on the show bench in 1955.

'Holyrood'

Another variety from the House of Douglas. It was raised in 1985. The flowers produced on our plants could only be classed as poor, but our stock receives no special treatment or supplementary feeding; it may perform properly when grown well. (See photo on page 8.)

'Jack Wood'

A 'Fleminghouse' seedling raised by David Hadfield in the early 1980s. 'Jack Wood' won the Corsar Cup in 1983, but it is a very rare variety, as it dies easily even with the most experienced grower. This is not one for the beginner.

'Gretna Green'

'Haffner'

'Hew Dalrymple'

'Jupiter'

'John'

This variety has a light green edge. It was raised by Dr Robert Newton, in 1962.

'Julia'

'Julia' was raised by Les Rollason, in 1976, from a 'Chloë' and 'Geldersome Green' cross. It was exhibited in 1992.

'Jupiter'

This variety has a lighter green than many of the other green edges. It was raised by David Hadfield in 1979 from 'Fleminghouse' seed and won two Premiers in 1992.

'Marmion'

Shown in 1950, though as a grey edge, this variety

was raised by James Douglas senior in 1901. Even in the 1950s this plant had very little farina – just enough to class it as a grey. It is quite small and offsets readily. The plant we grow under this name has very little farina, if any, which is why we list it as a green; 'Marmion' is also listed by other nurseries as a green edge.

'Mary of Doonhill'

Raised by Stan Kos, in 1975, and named after his wife, Mary, who was in the house, 'doonhill' from the garden. It was shown in 1975.

'Mary Taylor'

Another green from the Douglas stable. 'Mary Taylor' was raised in 1969.

'Nappa Tandy'

Raised by Jack Ballard in 1969 from a 'Serenity' and 'James Stockhill' cross. Exhibited in 1985.

'Oban'

An easy green which offsets fairly readily and produces quite a presentable truss with little effort. Raised by Gordon Douglas in the 1980s.

'Orb'

This fine plant was raised by Dr D. A. Duthie in 1962 from a 'James Stockhill' and 'Bisterne' cross. The edge is a distinctive olive green. It produces a reasonable number of offsets, is not difficult to grow, and can be magnificent on its day. 'Orb' is regularly seen on the show bench.

'Paris'

A green edge raised by David Hadfield, in 1978, from 'Fleminghouse' seed. 'Paris' was awarded the Corsar Cup when it was shown in 1981.

'Peter Klein'

A North American plant, bred by Peter Klein in the 1950s, the result of crossing a grey and a green that

'Marmion'

he had raised from Haysom seed. It was awarded the Bamford Trophy in 1957 at the show of the American Primrose Society.

'Prague'

An excellent lightish green that shows well. Raised by David Hadfield from 'Chloë' and 'Fleminghouse' seed and awarded the Corsar Cup in 1976. It is reckoned one of the best, with large, well-proportioned pips which come flat and round, building up a splendid truss. 'Prague' is probably the most frequently exhibited green edge.

'Roberto'

A fine plant bred by Dr Robert Newton, in 1966, from a 'John' and 'Teem' cross. With skilful growing and a bit of luck, it can make a fine, large truss of beautifully formed pips. Unfortunately, it offsets very slowly, if at all, so tends not to be available. After more than 10 years of growing this variety we still have only two plants. It has been a regular prizewinner in recent years.

'Scipio'

This variety, with a pale green edge, will probably

'Oban'

'Orb'

'Paris'

'Prague'

need drastic thinning to produce a plant worthy of showing. It was raised by David Hadfield and shown in 1988. (See photo on page 45.)

'Serenity'

This easy and reliable plant is not really of show quality. It was raised by Jack Ballard, in 1957, from Haysom seed and shown in 1960. Though the top

showmen in Britain class it as not worth growing, it is held in high regard in the USA. 'Serenity' is an excellent plant for beginners, and those who have no aspirations to exhibit. (See photo over page.)

'Shirley Hibberd'

A living piece of history, 'Shirley Hibberd' is the oldest green-edged Show still in existence. It was

'Serenity'

'Tinkerbell'

raised by Ben Simonite in 1897. Unfortunately, though not surprisingly, its form has deteriorated badly over the years, and it was last shown in 1963. It has now been micro-propagated in order to save it from extinction.

'Superb'

This variety has a light green edge. Raised by Fred Buckley, in 1962. 'Superb' appeared on the show bench in 1967.

'Tinkerbell'

This difficult plant was raised by Clive Cookson in 1932. It tends to look half dead in winter, often hanging on with one miserable root. 'Tinkerbell' has been micropropagated, but this hasn't made it any easier.

'Tye Lea'

A green edge raised by Mrs Tye of Lea Rhododendron Gardens in Derbyshire, England.

GREY EDGED

'Almondbury'

An attractive grey of fairly good form. 'Almondbury' was raised from a tray of seedlings given by Jack Stant to another grower around 1970, and exhibited in 1980. It was named after an area of Huddersfield, in Yorkshire, England.

'Clare'

A very fine grey edge. This variety was raised by

Peter Ward, in 1980, from a 'Walhampton' and 'Helena' cross. Vigorous and reliable, it can be an excellent show plant on its day, though it is liable to distort if overfed.

'Cornmeal'

Cy Happy raised this interesting North American plant in the 1970s. It is not really a grey edge as the dusting of meal on the petals has a distinct yellow

'Almondbury'

'Embley'

'Emery Down'

'Grey Lag'

cast, as reflected in its name. 'Cornmeal' offsets generously and produces a good head of flowers with minimal care.

'Embley'

This variety is an old and little-known Haysom grey that was seen on the show bench in 1952. It is probably past its best.

'Emery Down'

An attractive grey edge which is not often grown. It was raised by C. G. Haysom, and shown in 1966. 'Emery Down' was named after a village in the New Forest, Hampshire, England.

'Grey Hawk'

An excellent grey raised by David Hadfield, in 1988,

'Helena'

'Lovebird'

from a 'Hawkwood' and unnamed fancy cross. It has been awarded two Premiers but, sadly, lacks vigour. It is a true grey with a leaden look to the meal on the edges of the pips.

'Grey Lag'

This variety, with attractive foliage, performs quite well on the show bench. Raised by Jack Ballard and first shown in 1969. (See photo on page 125.)

'Grey Seal'

Now considered inferior to the modern greys, this variety was raised by Dr Robert Newton in 1966. It appeared on the show bench in 1980.

'Helena'

This variety has a rich yellow tube and well-mealed, serrated leaves. It can be an excellent grey when grown well, and has won two Premiers. 'Helena' was bred by Fred Buckley in 1968.

'Jessica'

A beautiful grey edge given to Dr Newton, by C. G. Haysom, as an unflowered seedling. Of unknown

parentage, but from Haysom's own seed. First shown in 1994, it has won many Premier Awards, receiving one as late as the mid-1980s. Together with 'Teem', an outstanding grey of the 1950s and 1960s. Although very scarce, it has been micro-propagated, and may make a comeback.

'Lovebird'

A reliable old grey with neat foliage, raised by James Douglas in 1908. It has neat, serrated leaves and small, seven-petalled pips of good form. 'Lovebird' makes an occasional appearance on the show bench.

'Ludlow'

A small but beautiful grey raised by Ed Pickin. First shown in 1983, 'Ludlow' won the Corsar Cup in 1986. Its parents are 'Embley' and 'Teem'.

'Queen's Bower'

An old grey raised by C. G. Haysom in 1947 and exhibited in 1956. While not of show quality, it will occasionally surprise you by producing a top-quality head of flowers. It was named after a village on the Isle of Wight. (See photo on page 128.)

'Ludlow'

'Rosalie Edwards'

An attractive grey that was given to Dennis Edwards as a seedling; he named it after his daughter. It can be good, but is very fickle. (See photo over page.)

'Saint Boswells'

An excellent grey with very attractive foliage, raised by Ron Cole in 1972 from a 'Sea Fret' and 'Teem' cross. First shown in 1975.

'Sherwood'

Another from the House of Douglas; a pleasant, easy, grey edge, just short of show class. It is occasionally seen on the show bench.

'Teem'

One of the best and most reliable greys, this well-known variety has stood the test of time. Raised by Thomas Meek from Haysom seed and first shown in

'Queen's Bower'

'Rosalie Edwards'

'Teem'

'Warwick'

1957. An elegant plant, it can be classed as either grey or white. It is a good variety for showing and has been used extensively in breeding programs.

'Tenby Grey'

Purchased as an unflowered seedling from a nursery near Tenby, South Wales, in the early 1970s. It was exhibited at the 1992 Southern Section Show.

'Warwick'

'Warwick' is an excellent grey-edged Show. It was bred by Peter Ward, in 1976, from a 'Walhampton' and 'Teem' cross. The flowers have a thin, black body and a good grey edge. This very refined plant is classed as one of the best. Grown well it can be unbeatable, however, careful attention must be paid to feeding and thinning, and it does tend to be somewhat late flowering.

GREY/WHITE EDGED

'Ben Lawers'

A variety raised by Gordon Douglas, around 1981. 'Ben Lawers' is a vigorous plant with exceptionally fine foliage. It can be classed either as a grey edge or a white edge.

'Ben Wyves'

Another plant from the House of Douglas. This variety was raised in the 1980s.

'Brookfield'

This is an attractive and vigorous plant. It was raised by Peter Ward, in 1979, from an F2 seedling from a 'Walhampton' and 'Teem' cross. It was exhibited in 1985. 'Brookfield' has a smooth, dense paste, and can be classed as either a grey or white edge. It is a good variety when well grown.

'Candida'

A variety raised by W. R. Hecker, in 1972, from a 'Lovebird' and 'Patriot' cross.

'Colbury'

An old and, unfortunately, unreliable variety. 'Colbury' was raised by C. G. Haysom in 1960, and shown in 1961.

'Dovedale'

Raised by Arthur Delbridge.

'Elegance'

This variety has large leaves that are attractively mealed. However, it is not the easiest plant to grow well and it rarely achieves show class; it is a plant for the experienced grower. 'Elegance' was raised by Fred Buckley prior to 1968.

'Falsefields'

The naming of this variety provides an interesting story. It is thought to be a plant that was, at first, incorrectly circulated as 'Fairfield', and was subsequently renamed 'Falsefield'. It appeared on the show bench in 1971.

'Brookfield'

'Elegance'

'Grey Friar'

'Maggie'

'Gavin Ward'

A very good and reliable variety that was raised by Peter Ward, in 1976, from a 'Walhampton' and 'Teem' cross. It was named after his son. Unfortunately it is not widely available as very few offsets are produced.

'George Rudd'

Thomas Woodhead raised this famous plant in 1882. It was losing its vigour and had become very scarce but has now been micropropagated and hopefully will be available in the future.

'Grey Friar'

This is a useful plant for producing hybrids. Bred by Mr Buckley in the 1960s, it has now been superseded by better plants. Unfortunately the pips do not flatten properly, but the tube, paste and body colour are excellent. It was seen on the show bench in 1980.

'Grey Tarquin'

A late-flowering variety of very good form. Raised by Trevor Newton in 1982, from a 'Fleminghouse' and 'Elegance' cross.

'Hetty Woolf'

'Hetty Woolf' is an easy and free-flowering variety that can be classed as either a grey or a white edge. It was raised by Kath Dryden, who named it after her grandmother.

'Jack Stant'

'Jack Stant' is an interesting white edge of somewhat obscure origins. It is a very heavily mealed variety.

'John Woolf'

Another variety raised by Kath Dryden, this one was named after her grandfather.

'Maggie'

As can be seen from the photo above, this is an attractive and free-flowering edge. 'Maggie' was raised by Allan Hawkes, in 1966, from a seedling and 'Somerley' cross.

'Magpie'

Raised by Fred Buckley in the 1960s, this variety was seen on the show bench in 1970.

'Silverway'

'Snowy Owl'

'The Bride'

'Victoria'

'Manka'

A difficult plant to keep healthy, this variety was bred by Jack Ballard in 1966 and shown in 1968. Its parents are 'White Parish' and 'W. Eckersley'.

'Margaret Martin'

Though it can occasionally be excellent, 'Margaret Martin' is, unfortunately, very unreliable. It is the offspring of a 'Teem' and 'Lovebird' cross, and was raised by Arthur J. Martin in 1973. In 1974 it was awarded the Corsar Cup.

'Pearl Diver'

This variety is a lovely grey/white edge. 'Pearl Diver' was raised by Les Kaye, around 1981, and was shown in 1983.

'Ray's Grey'

This variety was raised by Ray Downard of Chatham in the early 1990s.

'Silverway'

An attractive grey/white edge of unknown origin. It is vigorous and easy, but not of show quality. (See photo on page 131.)

'Slioch'

An easy plant that tends to produce many offsets, to the detriment of the main rosette. Raised by James Douglas. Seen on the show bench in 1982.

'Snowy Owl'

This variety, shown in 1986, can be either white or grey edged. 'Snowy Owl' is very similar to 'Teem'. (See photo on page 131.)

'The Bride'

A well-known plant that can be either grey or white edged, bred by Fred Buckley. It has the richest jet-black ground of any edges, rivalled only by 'Teem'. Unfortunately, it is often ruined by the whole flower, centre paste and ground, becoming a pentagon. 'The Bride' responds well to good growing and on its day can be excellent.

'Trojan'

Raised by James Douglas around 1930.

'Victoria'

A relatively unknown edge raised by David Hadfield. First shown in 1980. (See photo on page 131.)

'Yorkshire Grey'

A fine variety, bred by Allan Hawkes in 1970.

WHITE EDGED

'Aviemore'

Raised by Gordon Douglas in 1981.

'C. G. Haysom'

An old and reliable white edge with attractive, well-mealed leaves. Raised by R. Loake in 1962 from a 'George Rudd' seedling. An excellent variety that has stood the test of time, 'C. G. Haysom' regularly appears on the show bench.

'Douglas White'

A white edge raised by Gordon Douglas.

'James Arnot'

An attractive white edge with lovely foliage; a very popular plant that is regularly exhibited. Raised by Thomas Meek in 1961 from a 'Gloria' and 'J. W. Midgley' cross.

'Minstrel'

Les Wright raised this brilliantly white edge in 1986, from Douglas seed. It was shown in 1987.

'Sharman's Cross'

Attractive white edge raised by Peter Ward, in 1976, from a 'Walhampton' and 'Teem' cross. In great demand, it doesn't offset freely so is fairly scarce.

'Snow Lady'

Rae Berry raised this beautiful North American plant from English seed in the 1930s. Despite producing offsets only slowly, this plant has been grown continuously in the USA since then.

'Walhampton'

This variety, an old white edge, has proved to be very useful for breeding purposes, being the mother

'C. G. Haysom'

'James Arnot'

'Sharman's Cross'

'White Ensign'

of 'Warwick' and a number of other lovely greys from Peter Ward. 'Walhampton' was raised by C. G. Haysom in 1946, and named after a village near Lymington in Hampshire, England. It can be a bit straggly and difficult to get to flower well. (See photo on page 10.)

'White Ensign'

This variety has an attractive flower and heavily mealed foliage. 'White Ensign' was raised by James Douglas, and was shown in 1950.

'White Wings'

This can be very good or very bad. Raised by James Douglas in the 1930s. It has a tendency to produce many small offsets; to flower well, these need to be removed so that there is just one strong rosette.

FANCIES

FOR MANY YEARS fancy auriculas have been classed as unworthy of the true Florists' interest, and as such they have been sadly neglected. I find the fancies some of the most fascinating and beautiful of the auriculas. At the shows they always arouse interest and admiration, especially among novice growers.

Fancies are normally pot-grown in a cold greenhouse with the other Shows, although many of the more vigorous green and red fancies, such as 'Rolts', are very garden worthy.

ORIGINS

From the auricula's earliest days there have been plants called 'fancies'. This was first used as a general term to describe any auricula that was not plain. However, over the years these 'fancies' were renamed 'edges' and 'stripes',

and the term 'fancy' fell into obscurity, resurfacing as a term used for failed edges. The Northern Section of the National Auricula and Primula Society are working towards lifting the fancy above its previous standing as a 'failed edge'. They are also very interested in re-introducing the 'painted ladies' and 'bizarres' of yesteryear.

Painted ladies and bizarres were the favoured types of auricula during the first half of the eighteenth century. As far as we can tell – from contemporary descriptions and paintings – they had multi-coloured petals, usually red and yellow variegated, covered with a scattering of farina across the face of the pip.

The term 'painted lady' probably derives from the use of coloured cosmetics and white face powder by ladies of fashion. 'Bizarre' appears simply a Continental equivalent of 'painted lady'.

From the mid-eighteenth century onwards, these varieties were superseded, due to the development of the edged Show auriculas that we know today.

RECOMMENDED VARIETIES

'Astolat'

'Grey Monarch'

'Hawkwood'

'Lisa Clara'

'Rajah'

'Sweet Pastures'

'Sweet Pastures'

DESCRIPTION

A fancy is described as being a Show auricula that does not conform to the standards for any of the other classes. They are usually edges (green, grey or white) with the body of a colour other than black, for example, red, yellow, purple or blue. However, under the Northern Standards (see Appendix 1, page 169), if the edge is of sufficient quality, and the body colour is bright and clear, the plant may be classed as an edge.

'Astolat'

'Clunie II'

'Coffee'

'Colonel Champney'

'Astolat'

An easy and rewarding plant that was raised by
W. R. Hecker around 1971. The refined flowers have
a mauve-pink to light red body colour and a light
green edge. 'Astolat' produces plenty of offsets.

'Bramshill'

'Bramshill' is a red-and-green fancy, one of the
many good fancies to come from the House of
Douglas. Curiously, it was named after the Police
College of Bramshill.

'Broughton'

Another good green-and-red fancy from the House
of Douglas, this variety is classed as one of the best.
'Broughton' appeared on the show bench in 1988.

'Daftie Green'

'Donna Clancy'

'Claudia Taylor'

A red-and-green fancy. Raised by Gordon Douglas, in 1985, from a 'Rolts' and 'Rajah' cross.

'Clunie II'

A vigorous, easy cerise-and-green fancy. Raised by Gordon Douglas, in 1985, from a 'Rolts' and 'Rajah' cross. (Its namesake, 'Clunie I', was a green-edged show, but this plant is now probably extinct.) (See photo on page 135.)

'Coffee'

This attractive plant was raised by Gwen Baker, in 1977, from a 'Lovebird' and 'Teem' cross, and shown in 1980. It has a good white ring of paste, a pale, milky coffee body merging into green, and a grey edge. (See photo on page 135.)

'Colonel Champney'

One of the oldest auriculas in cultivation, this variety was raised by W. Turner in 1867. It is a vigorous plant, but has very poor-quality blooms, with too much body and hardly any edge. The body is dark maroon-purple and the narrow edge is grey. (See photo on page 135.)

'Conservative'

A grey-and-red fancy from the House of Douglas. Seen on the show bench in 1963.

'Crimple'

This is one of the new generation of fancies from Tim Coop. 'Crimple' is an incredibly beautiful plant in mauve-blue and green – it could almost be classed as a stripe.

'Daftie Green'

Dark, rich purple body with a very narrow green edge, often lightly mealed on the very tip. 'Daftie Green' is quite a small plant.

'Donna Clancy'

A vigorous and easy red-and-green that offsets freely. Raised by Gordon Douglas, in 1985, from a 'Rolts' and 'Rajah' cross.

'Eileen K'

A beautiful yellow-and-green fancy. 'Eileen K' was raised by John Kemp, in the late 1980s, and named after his mother.

'Eileen K'

'Error'

'Glenelg'

'Green Isle'

'Elmor Vete'

A green-and-red fancy from the House of Douglas. Named after a nurse.

'Error'

An unusual colour, the small flowers have a purple-blue ground and a narrow grey edge. It was raised by Allan Guest and was one of a pair – 'Trial' and 'Error' – named after he had carefully made deliberate crosses and raised the seedlings, then moved house and mixed them all up! The trial died. 'Error' was exhibited in 1986.

'Frank Taylor'

A yellow-and-grey fancy from the House of Douglas. Raised in 1974 and named after Dr Frank Taylor of Wye College, in Kent, England.

'Greta'

'Grey Monarch'

'Glenelg'

Raised in 1974 from a 'Rolts' seedling from the House of Douglas. An easy, dark, red-and-green fancy. (See photo on page 137.)

'Grace Ellen'

A green-and-red fancy. Raised by Gordon Douglas, in 1985, from a 'Rolts' and 'Rajah' cross.

'Green Isle'

This red-and-green fancy was raised by James Douglas around 1930. (See photo on page 137.)

'Green Shank'

One of the older red-and-green fancies. It appeared on the show bench in 1970.

'Greenpeace'

A green-and-yellow fancy raised by John Fielding.

'Greta'

'Greta' is a lovely and vigorous fancy raised by J. F. Robinson in 1926. It has lots of relatively small pips

and a light orange-red body with a narrow, light green edge. This variety would probably benefit from the pips being thinned.

'Grey Monarch'

'Grey Monarch' is a good variety that was raised by James Douglas and seen on the show bench in 1959. It is still a very healthy and reliable plant that offsets steadily and is relatively easy to grow. With its golden-yellow body and grey edge, it is a very eye-catching plant.

'Grey Shrike'

Another beautiful grey-edged fancy, this variety has a rich yellow body. 'Grey Shrike' is not as easy to grow as 'Grey Monarch', but the results are well worth the effort. It was raised by Gordon Douglas and exhibited in 1982.

'Hawkwood'

This classic fancy has a dark red body with a reasonable grey edge. It was raised by James Douglas and shown in 1970. Like 'Grey Monarch', 'Hawkwood' offsets readily and is a relatively easy plant to grow.

'Grey Shrike'

'Hawkwood'

'Hinton Admiral'

'Hinton Fields'

'Hazel's Fancy'

This is an attractive red-and-grey variety, raised by Hazel Blackburn.

'Helen Barter'

Originally named 'Helen Mary'. An unusual fancy with a purple-blue body and a green edge. It was raised by Roy Barter, President of the Southern Section of the National Auricula and Primula Society, and named after his daughter.

'Hinton Admiral'

This variety seems to have deteriorated over the years – the plant in cultivation has a dark red body and a narrow white edge while the plant pictured in the 1950 yearbook of the National Auricula and

'Lisa Clara'

'Margaret'

Primula Society has an attractive grey/white edge. 'Hinton Admiral' was raised by C. G. Haysom in 1937 and named after a village south of the New Forest in Hampshire, England.

'Hinton Fields'

A lovely fancy with a bright yellow body and green edge. It was raised by A. J. Martin from a 'Spring Meadows' natural cross. 'Hinton Fields' first appeared on the show bench in 1967. (See photo on page 139.)

'Idmiston'

A green-and-red fancy that is vigorous and easy, from the House of Douglas.

'Lady Emma Monson'

This is another 'Rolts' and 'Rajah' seedling from Gordon Douglas, raised in 1983. It has a red body and green edge.

'Laverock Fancy'

A green-and-red 'Rolts' seedling raised by Gordon Douglas in 1983. (See photo on page 29.)

'Lisa Clara'

'Lisa Clara' is another green-and-red fancy from the House of Douglas. It is an easy plant to grow. Introduced in 1985, it was named after Brenda Hyatt's granddaughter.

'Mansell's Green'

An old Douglas seedling of very poor form. It was once classed as a green-edged show but has deteriorated badly over the years.

'Margaret'

'Margaret' is a lovely, bright, green-and-yellow fancy. It was raised by Mrs Beedham in 1993 and named after a friend.

'Minley'

A cerise-and-green fancy with distinct serrated foliage. Raised by Gordon Douglas in 1982. This is an easy plant that offsets well.

'Number 21'

A very refined fancy of unknown origin. It has a dark red body and a grey edge.

'Number 21'

'Queen Bee'

'Rajah'

'Rondy'

'Old England'

A lovely grey-and-red fancy with the broad edge that modern breeders are trying to introduce. It was raised by Jack Robson of Newcastle.

'Parakeet'

A striking North American fancy described as a strange combination of green, yellow and white.

'Patricia Barras'

Another variety of green-and-red fancy from the House of Douglas.

'Portree'

'Portree' is a vigorous, easy and bright, red-and-green fancy. It was raised in 1984 from a 'Rolts' and 'Rajah' cross.

141

'Spring Meadows'

'Star Wars'

'Queen Bee'

'Queen Bee' is a lovely fancy with a rich crimson body and a good grey edge. Raised by Hazel Blackburn in 1984. One of the finest of the fancies, 'Queen Bee' is always in great demand. (See photo on page 141.)

'Rajah'

Combining a body of bright scarlet-red with a green edge and a small paste centre, this is an eye-catching plant, which offsets readily. Raised by James Douglas in the 1950s and exhibited in 1964. (See photo on page 141.)

'Redstart'

The true 'Redstart' was raised by Dr D. A. Duthie, in 1962, from Douglas seed. It is now probably extinct. The plant now in circulation under the name is not the true 'Redstart'.

'Rolts'

This is an easy, vigorous plant with a red body and a green edge. It is vigorous enough for the garden, and has the potential to win prizes. It was raised by A. C. Rolt in 1894.

'Rondy'

An attractive green-and-yellow, raised in Scotland, and exhibited in 1988. (See photo on page 141.)

'Salad'

A yellow-and-green fancy with a white edge. Raised by Thomas Meek from a 'Spring Meadows' and 'Ower' cross. It was exhibited in 1966.

'Shrewton'

This variety is a grey-and-yellow fancy from the House of Douglas.

'Space Age'

Another desirable fancy, from Tim Coop of Harrogate, England, this plant has the same parentage as 'Star Wars'.

'Spring Meadows'

A strong plant that offsets well. The yellow-and-green fancies are always very popular, and the sparklingly bright colour combination of this variety is very eye-catching. Raised by Jack Ballard in 1957. Appeared on the show bench in 1962.

'Sweet Pastures'

'Tosca'

'Star Wars'

This is a lovely purple-and-grey fancy. It is a vigorous plant and is easy to grow. 'Star Wars' was raised by Tim Coop from a cross between a pin-eyed, purple-bodied seedling and a grey edge. We grow two clones of 'Star Wars'; while these are very slightly different in habit, the flowers of the plants are identical.

'Stubb's Tartan'

This variety has a huge, flat flower with a red body and a grey edge. 'Stubb's Tartan' was raised by Alec Stubbs. It was shown in 1975.

'Sweet Pastures'

This fancy was raised by Jack Ballard in 1957 and shown in 1964. As can be seen in the photo above, 'Sweet Pastures' has large flowers with a yellow body and grey edge.

'Swinley'

A grey-and-yellow fancy introduced by the House of Douglas in the 1970s.

'Tosca'

A vigorous and easy green-and-red fancy. 'Tosca' was raised by Gordon Douglas in 1984 from a 'Rolts' and 'Rajah' cross.

'Wexland'

A strong variety with an orange-yellow body and a silver-grey edge. A highly desirable plant that offsets steadily. Raised by the House of Douglas in the 1970s. It won a Premier in 1977.

'Yelverton'

A lovely grey-and-yellow fancy from the House of Douglas. Introduced in the mid 1970s.

SELFS

ORIGINS

The selfs probably date from the early part of the nineteenth century, but it is very difficult to sort out whether the Alpine (previously called a 'self' or a 'shaded self') or the self as it is known today is being referred to in auricula records.

Selfs were very popular in the second half of the nineteenth century, but in the first half of the twentieth, were more or less ignored.

In the last 50 years many new varieties have been bred and there is now a bewildering choice of lovely selfs. Recently several growers

'Goldenhill'; an attractive yellow that offsets readily

have been working on the breeding of new selfs in different colours; examples include the glorious 'Blue Steel' from Brian Coop.

RECOMMENDED VARIETIES

Red
'Red Gauntlet'

Yellow
'Golden Fleece'

Blue
'Remus'

'Red Gauntlet'

Dark
'Nocturne'

Other
'Rosebud'
'Moonglow'
'Purple Sage'

'Moonglow'

DESCRIPTION

The selfs are Show auriculas with an even body colour from the paste edge to the petal margin; there is no shading and no edge. They are subdivided into red, yellow, blue, dark and other, according to their body colour.

REDS

'Alfred Niblett'

A fairly old variety with neat pips of dusky red. It has now been superseded by the modern reds. Bred by Hal Cohen in the early 1960s, from Haysom seed. Shown in 1964.

'Alice Haysom'

A dark cardinal red self, raised by C. G. Haysom and Hew Dalrymple in 1935. It has good form, but the paste is a bit coarse.

'American Beauty'

A North-American self bred by Beth Tait. Mid-red, good form and a bold head of pips on a sturdy stem.

'Bali Hi'

A red self, raised by Derek Telford around 1978.

'Blackfield'

A red self. Raised by C. G. Haysom in 1960.

'Cherry'

A distinct plant that was bred by Dr D. A. Duthie, in 1968, from a cross between 'Harrison Weir' and HMR1 (a 'The Mikado' x 'Rosalind' seedling). First appeared on the show bench in 1969. It has good form, offsets freely and, if the buds are removed, is an excellent variety for the beginner. Aptly named, the colour is cherry red. This plant is generally either loved or hated.

'Cheyenne'

One of the best of the darker reds, and an excellent plant. Raised by Peter Ward, in 1971, from a cross between 'Pat' and HMR1 (a 'The Mikado' x 'Rosalind' seedling). This variety has a tendency to flower early, and its attractively mealed foliage tends to yellow in autumn. 'Cheyenne' offsets freely.

'Chiricahua'

Another red raised by Peter Ward, in 1973, from a cross between 'Pat' and HMR1 (a 'The Mikado' x 'Rosalind' seedling).

'Alfred Niblett'

'Cheyenne'

'Favourite'

'Geronimo'

'Connie'

Another red raised by Derek Telford, in 1975.

'Cortina'

A good red of a velvety texture, with very attractive foliage. Raised by Derek Telford. It appeared on the show bench in 1983.

'Fanny Meerbeck'

An easy, vigorous plant of a good bright red. 'Fanny Meerbeck' is an old variety, raised by Ben Simonite of Sheffield, England, in 1898. It appears on the show bench occasionally.

'Favourite'

A good, bright red of sturdy constitution. Probably raised by Ben Simonite, in 1904. It is an excellent beginners' plant.

'Geronimo'

A fine, dark red variety that can be recognized in winter by its lovely golden farina. Raised by Peter Ward, in 1971, from the same parents as 'Cheyenne' and 'Chiricahua'.

'Grizedale'

A rich, bright red with messy, unmealed leaves, somewhat similar to 'The Mikado'. Raised by A. E. G. Kilshaw around 1972.

'Hardley'

A darkish red bred by C. G. Haysom. Seen on the show bench in 1958.

'Harrison Weir'

A famous variety raised by James Douglas senior in 1908, named after a well-known animal painter and cat breeder of that time. It has been superseded by the excellent new reds that have been bred over the last 30 years.

'Harry "O"'

A dark, maroon-red self with heavily mealed, attractive foliage. Raised by Tim Coop in 1985.

'Headdress'

Derek Telford raised this variety in 1978, and it was shown in 1980. The colour tends very slightly towards cherry red.

'Grizedale'

'Harry "O"'

'Lechistan'

'Lich'

'Kiowa'

Very bright orange-red. Raised by Peter Ward, in 1976, from a 'Pat' and ('Pat' x 'HMR1') cross. Small, well-shaped pips and neat, heavily mealed foliage.

'Lady Zoë'

This red self was raised by Jack Wemyss-Cooke in 1982, from a 'The Mikado' and 'Nocturne' cross.

'Lechistan'

A good, bright red with finely serrated, well-mealed leaves. Raised by Stan Kos in 1983 and exhibited in 1985. An excellent beginners' plant as it is easy and undemanding, has good colour and offsets readily.

'Lich'

This variety is a very attractive shade of light red,

with well-mealed foliage. It is of unknown origin. (See photo on page 147.)

'Lisa's Red'

This plant is a good, reliable, darkish red self. 'Lisa's Red' was bred by Derek Telford and shown in 1985. It was named after his granddaughter, as was 'Lisa's Smile' (see description on page 152).

'Mandan'

'Mandan' is another of the many red selfs from Peter Ward. He raised it, in 1976, from a 'Pat' and HMR1 F2 cross.

'Matley'

This red self was raised by C. G. Haysom.

'Mojave'

'Mojave'

The body colour of this self is a lovely light red, as shown in the photo, above right. It was raised by Peter Ward and exhibited in 1980.

'Neville Telford'

'Neville Telford' is a good, reliable red. It was raised by Derek Telford, in 1978, and named after his brother. This variety is often a prizewinner when it is well grown.

'Old Red Elvet'

'Old Red Elvet' is a red self of unknown origin. 'Elvet' means 'tiny elf' (*Elfland*, T. P. Battersby, 1825). This variety has all the appearance of an antique plant and could well date back to the nineteenth century.

'Pat'

This classic standard is acknowledged as one of the best red selfs. It was bred by J. Ballard, in 1966, from a 'Pimadel' and 'Adonis' cross. The foliage is attractive and well-mealed. 'Pat' is said to be prone to root rot, so it is probably safer to keep it slightly drier than other varieties. It has proved to be a very useful parent in recent years.

'Red Beret'

This variety is Derek Telford's best red, and has proved consistently good for showing. It is a small plant and has neat, beautifully mealed leaves with no serrations; the blooms are small and perfect. It was raised in 1976.

'Red Gauntlet'

This variety is a bright, soft red self. It was raised by Dr D. A. Duthie, in 1968, from a cross between a red seedling and HMR1 (a 'The Mikado' and 'Rosalind' seedling). It was awarded the Corsar Cup in 1969. The foliage is tinged slightly yellow, and it offsets freely. 'Red Gauntlet' is an excellent, easy plant which, with due care and attention, can produce a show winner.

'Red Rum'

A dark red variety with attractive foliage. 'Red Rum' was bred by Derek Telford and named for the famous Grand National winner. Shown in 1985. Not the easiest to keep healthy.

'Rosemary'

A dark, brownish red self of unknown origin.

'Neville Telford'

'Red Beret'

'Red Gauntlet'

'Shere'

'Shere'

A lovely, early-flowering, lightish red variety. Bred by K. J. Gould, in 1966, from a 'Fanny Meerbeck' and 'Adonis cross'. Exhibited in 1970.

'The Bishop'

Raised by Stan Kos in 1974 from a 'Melody' and 'Alice Haysom' cross.

'Trudy'

Dark red with attractive, well-mealed foliage. Bred by Derek Telford in the 1980s; named after his cousin. Same parentage as 'Gizabroon' (see page 158).

'Wor Jackie'

A dark red bred by Derek Telford. The name, after footballer Jackie Milburn, is Geordie for 'Our Jackie'.

YELLOWS

'Antoc'

A bright yellow variety of unknown origin, which appeared on the show bench in 1986. 'Antoc' is easy and reliable.

'April Moon'

This is a lovely pale yellow self from Tim Coop. It was raised in 1988 from a 'Moonglow' and 'Helen' cross. Hopefully it will become generally available in the future.

'Beauty of Bath'

An old yellow self that was raised by Ken Gould around 1960. We find that it is not the easiest of plants to keep healthy.

'Beckjay'

A yellow self, raised by Jack Ballard in 1972.

'Beeches...'

In the 1970s Lawrence Wigley, from Carshalton Beeches in Surrey, England, raised many yellow selfs using 'Melody' for pollen. Thirteen of the resultant plants were named using the prefix 'Beeches'. They are often to be seen at the shows of the Southern Section of the National Auricula and Primula Society.

'Bendigo'

A yellow self. Raised by James Douglas and exhibited in 1950.

'Bilton'

A good yellow with neat foliage. Bred by Derek Telford in the early 1970s.

'Bookham Star'

A yellow self, supposedly still vigorous. Raised by James Douglas in 1918.

'Brass Dog'

An old yellow variety raised by Dr Robert Newton.

'Brazil'

A good yellow with neat, well-mealed foliage. Bred by Derek Telford in 1981 and shown in 1982. It produces plenty of offsets.

'Brompton'

The best yellow self in circulation, it appears regularly on the show bench. Bred by David Hadfield in 1976 from a 'Goldilocks' and 'Melody' cross. It is somewhat slow to offset, so tends to be in short supply.

'Corntime'

A light yellow from Tim Coop. Raised in 1988 from a 'Moonglow' and 'Helen' cross.

'Elsinore'

A good beginners' plant of a rich yellow – vigorous and easy. Raised by Peter Ward in the mid-1970s from a 'Yellow Hammer' and 'Sunflower' cross.

'Gleam'

An easy, reliable plant, although not the best for showing. The flowers are a rich golden-yellow. Raised by James Douglas, it appeared on the show bench in 1954.

'Golden Fleece'

A wonderful yellow raised by Les Kaye from a 'Rock Sand' and 'Brompton' cross. It has excellent form, with almost perfect flowers. Awarded the Corsar Cup in 1988. Highly recommended.

'Goldenhill'

'Goldenhill' is a good yellow and the sister to 'Guinea' (see description opposite). It was raised by

'Antoc'

'Brompton'

'Golden Fleece'

'Goldenhill'

Dr D. A. Duthie, in 1971, from a 'Willowbrook' and 'Sunflower' cross. It is an attractive variety which offsets reasonably. Exhibited in 1972.

'Goldilocks'

This yellow is similar to 'Queen of Sheba' (see description on page 152), but with no meal on the leaves. Raised by F. Buckley in 1958.

'Guinea'

'Guinea' is a good yellow self for beginners, being both a vigorous and reliable plant. It also a variety that offsets readily, with the result that it is quite widely available. It was raised by Dr D. A. Duthie and, as mentioned before, it is a sister plant to 'Goldenhill' (see photo above and description on page 150). 'Guinea' is a very attractive plant, with heavily mealed foliage.

'Harvest Moon'

Les Rollason raised this reliable, pale yellow self in 1976, from a 'Rosebud' and 'Sunflower' F2 cross.

'Helen'

An attractive yellow raised by Tim Coop, in 1981, from a 'Douglas Old Gold' seedling and 'Chorister' cross. The foliage is mealed, but can be very messy at times. 'Helen' is a vigorous, easy plant, and makes a good parent.

'Leeside Yellow'

A small plant with a few canary-yellow pips. It was raised by Dr Robert Newton, in 1963, from a 'Melody' and 'Ower' cross.

'Lemon Drop'

'Lemon Drop' is an easy, lemon-yellow self. It was raised by Tim Coop, in 1984, from a 'Moonglow' and 'Helen' cross.

'Lisa's Smile'

The body colour of this variety is a lovely, bright, clear yellow. Bred by Derek Telford in 1982 and shown in 1983. A good plant for the beginner, it still regularly wins prizes.

'Mary Zac'

A yellow self from the USA, this is an attractive and easy variety. It was raised by Ivanel Agee. (See photo on page 13.)

'Melody'

A very important parent that was bred by C. G. Haysom and introduced in 1936. It has pale yellow, well-formed flowers with dense, clear white paste. A good show plant.

'Moneymoon'

A lovely, very pale yellow, with almost transparent petals. Bred by Tim Coop, in 1989, from a 'Moonglow' and 'Helen' cross.

'Helen'

'Pot o' Gold'

This is an attractive plant with neat foliage and deep yellow flowers. 'Pot o' Gold' was bred by Gwen Baker from a 'Chorister' and 'Sunflower' cross, and exhibited in 1983. It will offset very freely, so in order to achieve blooms that are of show quality, it is advisable to remove the offsets as soon as they form.

'Queen of Sheba'

'Queen of Sheba' is an old yellow self. It is not very vigorous, but could be of use in breeding. Raised by F. Buckley, in 1958.

'Sharon Louise'

This plant is a truly beautiful, late-flowering yellow self. 'Sharon Louise' was raised by Ken Bowser, in 1991, from a 'Brompton' and 'Upton Belle' cross. The large, beautifully shaped pips are of near perfect form.

'Sheila'

An attractive light yellow, vigorous, easy and good for showing. Bred by Allan Hawkes in 1961 and shown in 1966.

'Moneymoon'

'Sharon Louise'

'Sunflower'

'Tomboy'

'Sherbet Lemon'

A pale yellow self bred by Tim Coop, in 1984, from a 'Moonglow' and 'Helen' cross. Unfortunately, it is shy in producing offsets.

'Sunflower'

A vigorous and easy plant with good, bright yellow flowers. However, in hot weather these can age rapidly to an ugly dark gold. The leaves are moderately mealed. Recorded on the show bench in 1955, but otherwise of unknown origin. It has been listed as a parent of several yellow selfs.

'Sunstar'

A fine, true yellow self. 'Sunstar' was bred and shown by Les Kaye in 1982.

'The Baron'

This is a reasonable yellow. It was raised by J. Baxter and exhibited in 1980.

'Tomboy'

Another excellent yellow self from Tim Coop. He raised 'Tomboy' in 1984, from a 'Moonglow' and 'Helen' cross. It is somewhat late-flowering, and the paste does tend towards hexagonal, but it has won several prizes on the show bench. (See photo on page 153.)

'Tracy Ward'

A beautiful variety bred by Peter Ward, in 1976, from a 'Goldilocks' and 'Melody' cross. An excellent yellow with deep-coloured, thick petals, and the widest and smoothest paste of all the yellows.

'Upton Belle'

A very fine yellow. Raised by R. G. Rossiter, in 1974, from a 'Sunflower' and 'Chorister' cross. It has lovely, large, rich yellow pips and narrow, slightly serrated, lightly mealed leaves.

BLUES

'Ann Hill'

A good blue raised by C. F. Hill, in 1958, from a 'Blue Fire' and 'Fearless' cross. Shown in 1962. It is not readily available as it produces very few offsets.

'Blue Jean'

'Blue Jean' is a small, neat plant. It was raised by Derek Telford, in 1972, from a 'Stella' and 'Everest Blue' cross. It was named after his wife. The narrow leaves are only lightly mealed. When well grown, it carries a truss of small, mid-purple-blue, well-shaped flowers. It tends to be a much smaller plant than other auriculas.

'Blue Lagoon'

A blue variety raised by Les Rollason, in 1978, from a 'Blue Fire' cross.

'Blue Nile'

This is a small, attractive plant with neat, thickly mealed leaves and good, purple-blue pips. Bred by Robert Newton in 1962, from a 'Blue Fire' and 'Bloxham Blue' cross. It appeared on the show bench in 1968. 'Blue Nile' is a reliable plant, but small and slow in growth.

'Blue Steel'

A lovely light blue, distinct and very beautiful. Raised by Brian Coop from Douglas seed in the early 1980s and shown in 1986.

'Eventide'

This blue self is the result of an 'Everest Blue' and 'Remus' cross. It is one of a series of plants raised by Derek Telford from a batch of seed he received from John Gibson.

'Everest Blue'

A blue variety raised by Harold D. Hall, in 1959, from Haysom seed. Shown in 1960. A sturdy plant with lightly mealed foliage. It is good for breeding and offsets readily.

'Faro'

'Faro' is another blue from the same batch as 'Eventide' (see description above).

'Girl Guide'

This rich purple-blue self was introduced by K. Ellerton in 1971 and shown in the same year.

'Blue Nile'

'Blue Steel'

'Faro'

'Lepton Jubilee'

'Joel'

This is a fairly old blue self, raised by C. Bach in 1952. It is still in circulation.

'Lepton Jubilee'

A rich purple 'Blue Jean' seedling that was raised by John Gibson around 1977. 'Lepton Jubilee' was exhibited in 1983.

'Margaret Thatcher'

An excellent blue self bred by Jack Wemyss-Cooke and first shown in 1988.

'Martin Luther King'

This plant is sometimes known as 'MLK'. It is another blue from the same batch of seed as 'Eventide' and 'Faro'.

'Oake's Blue'

'Renata'

'Stant's Blue'

It has beautifully formed, rich purple-blue pips. Raised by Derek Telford, in 1974, from a 'Stella' and 'Everest Blue' cross. It was named after an area of Huddersfield, England. 'Oake's Blue' produces little petals from the tube in some years; a type of incipient doubling. This can just be seen in the uppermost left-hand pip in the photograph.

'Remus'

An old, reliable, purple-blue variety that is a good parent for breeding. Raised by W. R. Hecker, in the 1960s, from a Cookson seedling and 'Blue Fire' cross. Exhibited in 1967. It is still vigorous and offsets readily; it is advisable to remove the offsets as they form if you wish to show this plant.

'Renata'

A dark violet-blue variety. Bred by W. R. Hecker, in 1970, from a Cookson seedling and Douglas seedling cross. Exhibited in 1971. Not the easiest of plants to keep in good health.

'Sailor Boy'

Another purple-blue self. 'Sailor Boy' was raised by Jack Ballard, around 1968, from a 'Rosalind' and

'Midnight'

Another distinct plant from Derek Telford. The flowers are a beautiful rich dark blue, which could almost be described as navy. It tends to be a small plant, with attractive, well-mealed, neat leaves.

'Oake's Blue'

This is the best, most reliable blue in cultivation.

'Bloxham Blue' cross. It was exhibited in 1970. This variety produces a moderate number of offsets and is not a difficult plant.

'Stant's Blue'

This somewhat temperamental variety is more purple than the other blues. Raised by Jack Stant and shown in 1975.

'Stella'

A very attractive blue, bred by Robert Newton in 1965. Despite its poor growth habit, the good colour makes it useful for producing hybrids.

'Trumpet Blue'

Another plant from the same batch of seed as 'Eventide' (see description on page 154).

DARKS

'Barbarella'

A lovely plant, with a large truss of very dark red pips. Bred by Peter Ward in 1980. Its parents are 'Pat' and ('Rosalind' x 'The Mikado'). It has proved to be a top prizewinner.

'Blackhill'

A very dark red. Raised by Derek Telford, around 1978, from an 'Esthwaite' and dark self seedling cross. 'Blackhill' was exhibited in 1981, and can be very good.

'Consett'

A very dark red plant with lovely foliage. This variety tends to flower too early for the shows. It was raised by Derek Telford in 1973 from seed obtained from Robert Newton ('Neat and Tidy' x 'Adonis'). It was shown in 1974. 'Consett' is named after a town in the north-east of England. (See photo over page.)

'Dakota'

A fine, dark red bred by Derek Telford.

'Barbarella'

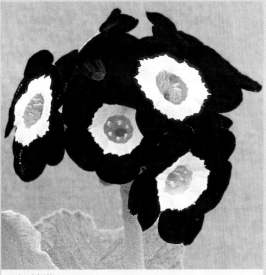

'Blackhill'

'Consett'

'Lindley'

'Douglas Black'

'Douglas Black' is an attractive dark self from the House of Douglas.

'Freda'

A dark self, raised by James Douglas prior to 1930, and listed in the Douglas catalogue in the 1960s.

'Gizabroon'

This variety is one of the lightest of the dark selfs. The body is almost a red, but there is a brownish cast to the colour, hence the name, which translates from the Geordie to 'give us a brown ale' (presumably, this means Newcastle Brown, an almost legendary drink in the north of England). 'Gizabroon' has glorious foliage, but it does tend to flower rather earlier than the other selfs. A regular plant on the show bench, it was bred by Derek Telford in 1974.

'Lindley'

A very dark, almost black self, and sister plant to 'The Snods' (see description on page 160). Derek Telford raised 'Lindley' in the late 1970s from an 'Esthwaite' and dark self seedling cross. It was exhibited in 1980.

'Neat and Tidy'

This nearly black self was raised by Dr Robert Newton in 1955, and shown in 1957. 'Neat and Tidy' is an excellent plant for the novice and has been winning prizes since it was first bred.

'Night and Day'

A very dark self raised by Derek Telford. Exhibited in 1980. It is a reliable and easy plant that performs well on the show bench.

'Nocturne'

This dark self, which is an excellent plant for the show bench, is often described as a refined 'Neat and Tidy'; it was raised from the same batch of seed by Dr Robert Newton, in 1957.

'Satchmo'

An excellent dark red. Raised by Derek Telford in 1978 from an 'Esthwaite' and dark self seedling cross. Exhibited in 1985.

'Super Para'

An excellent dark red. Bred by Derek Telford, in

'Neat and Tidy'

'Nocturne'

'Satchmo'

'Super Para'

1974, from a 'Neat and Tidy' and 'Nocturne' cross. An attractive reliable variety that is worth exhibiting.

'The Mikado'

This variety has very dark red to black flowers of a beautiful form. Raised by William Smith in 1906, and first listed by James Douglas in 1907. The floppy, light, yellow-green serrated leaves are

completely without meal. It is not easy to keep in good health, but has won more than its fair share of prizes over the years.

'The Raven'

This is another old variety raised by Ben Simonite, around 1900. It was first listed in the Douglas catalogue in 1926. The almost black flower of this

'Wincha'

variety is not of show standard – it has possibly deteriorated in quality over the years – but it is a vigorous, easy plant despite its age.

'The Snods'

This very dark red is a reasonable plant for the show bench. It is a sister plant to 'Lindley' (see description on page 158). Raised by Derek Telford in 1977 from an 'Esthwaite' and dark self seedling cross. Named after a hamlet in northern England.

'Wincha'

An attractive, very dark, almost black, self. The flowers can be of very good form, and the petals have an almost velvet appearance. Raised by Tim Coop from a 'Barbarella' and 'Harry "O"' cross, it was a prizewinning seedling.

OTHERS

'Black Ice'

Dark purplish brown. An interesting plant with lovely foliage but poor form. Raised in Norfolk.

'Chaffinch'

The pips of this plant open red and fade to a dark orange-pink, reminiscent of a chaffinch's breast. An attractive variety with lightly serrated foliage. It is reliable and easy.

'Chorister'

An old variety. Raised by A. Emlyn James and shown in 1967. It is a vigorous and easy plant with darkish, off-yellow flowers. 'Chorister' supposedly needs skill to make it flower, but ours manage. It produces plenty of offsets.

'Flamingo'

An interesting pink self. 'Flamingo' was raised by Derek Telford in 1980, from seed provided by David Hadfield ('Pat' x 'Moonglow').

'H80 Rose'

A lovely old rose self from the House of Douglas. The photo opposite illustrates how too many pips can ruin a display.

'H Old Gold'

An unusual rich bronze gold, this variety was raised by James Douglas.

'Humphrey'

A dark pink, almost red self, with rather small pips and neat foliage.

'Isabel'

A purple-blue self raised by Dr Robert Newton. 'Isabel' won the Corsar Cup in 1965. This variety is now very rare.

'Lilac Domino'

A purplish mauve self raised by Arthur Delbridge, in

'Chaffinch'

'Chorister'

'H80 Rose'

'H Old Gold'

the mid-1980s, from Dr Newton's seed. Not to be confused with the completely different *Primula* 'Lilac Domino'. (See photo over page.)

'Limelight'

A pale, greenish yellow self raised by Tim Coop, in the mid-1980s, from a 'Moonglow' and 'Moneymoon' cross. Exhibited in 1987.

'Moonglow'

This variety has a very, very pale, greenish yellow body colour. (See photo over page.) It was raised by David Hadfield, in 1975, from a 'Leeside Yellow' and 'Ower' cross. It was first exhibited in 1976, and since then has made regular appearances on the show bench. 'Moonglow' has also proved to be a useful parent; it is a parent of 'Flamingo' and 'Limelight' among others.

'Lilac Domino'

'Moonglow'

'Moonrise'

This variety opens yellow but ages to a very pale beige yellow. It was probably raised in the 1980s.

'Old Gold'

An unusual colour, described as chrome-yellow with a bronze tint. Raised by James Douglas prior to 1940. Possibly the same as 'H Old Gold'.

'Pink Lilac'

A purplish pink self with lovely foliage. This variety is of unknown origin.

'Pink Panther'

A rich pinkish purple self. Raised by Derek Telford in 1980, from the same batch of seed as 'Flamingo'.

'Purple Promise'

This cannot really be classed as a self as the petals do not lie flat and are slightly frilly, but it is a beautiful plant, with very distinctive, serrated, well-farinated foliage, which shows off the lightish purple blooms to perfection. I would recommend it for every collection, even though it is not fit for the show bench. Of unknown origin.

'Pink Lilac'

'Purple Sage'

A lovely rich purple self, a reliable and easy plant that always gives a good display. It was raised by Derek Telford in 1966.

'Rock Sand'

This variety is well named, being an unusual light, slightly off-yellow colour, though the grower, Les

'Purple Promise'

'Rock Sand'

'Rosebud'

'Sandmartin'

Kaye, names his plants after racehorses that win the Derby. Raised in 1982.

'Rosebud'

An excellent, dark pink self that is well worth growing. It has large, flat flowers, slightly marred by a suspicion of veining. Raised by James Douglas around 1940 and exhibited in 1955.

'Sandmartin'

An unusual dark golden sand colour, this is a lovely plant of unknown origin.

'Sugar Plum Fairy'

Another pinky purple self from the same batch of seed as 'Flamingo'.

STRIPES

ORIGINS

Striped auriculas were very popular until the second half of the eighteenth century, at which point they fell into disfavour, not to reappear until the 1960s. Again, their re-emergence was largely due to the work of the hybridizers.

Allan Hawkes was given a seedling which had a tendency towards stripes and, after many years of hybridization, began to produce seedlings with stripes.

Not only has Allan Hawkes been busy breeding and improving, Derek Parsons has also made enormous strides in resurrecting the range of colours that was available 250 years ago.

The number of varieties available is increasing by the year, and the striped auriculas now merit a class of their own at the shows. There are many wonderful new varieties being bred, but it does take time for them to be named and even longer for them to become generally available.

DESCRIPTION

In general, the standards for stripes are the same as for other Show auriculas, though at the time of writing, striped auriculas do not have the same form as the other Shows and some latitude is required in interpreting standards within their classes.

The stripes may be formed of meal and/or colour; the stripes should be radial, clearly defined and evenly spread; the stripes should not coalesce to form a body colour as in the edged forms.

As yet, many of the stripes have a very ragged outline; this is due mainly to the fact that their stripes are composed of two different constituents – they are part edge and part body – which grow at different speeds.

The varieties that have one body colour, with the stripe formed just by farina, present a much more rounded outline.

'April Tiger'

An attractive plant raised by Allan Hawkes, in 1985, from a 'Tiger Bay' and seedling cross. It has mauve stripes on a grey to white ground.

'Arundell'

This is a vigorous and easy plant that produces lots of offsets. It is irregularly striped in yellow, maroon-red and white. 'Arundell' was raised by Ray Downard, in 1986, from a pin-eyed seedling and 'Rajah' cross. The striping can vary considerably between pips on the same truss. Exhibited by Les Kaye at the 1993 Cheadle Show and awarded first prize in the striped class.

'Blackpool Rock'

A very pretty plant with pink and white stripes. Raised by Allan Guest, in 1988, from an 'Error' and 'Singer Stripe' cross. It can be difficult to keep healthy. (See photo over page.)

'Bob Tucker'

Gold and yellow stripes with a very irregular outline. Bred by Derek Parsons.

'Bold Tartan'

Bold, broad stripes in red and green. Raised by Judy Radford, in 1997, from seed provided by Allan Hawkes. A prizewinning seedling.

'Catherine Wheel'

Derek Parsons raised this prizewinning variety and named after his wife. It is brown and yellow with mealed stripes.

'Crinoline'

A beautiful plant raised by Tim Coop, with pale lavender and green stripes.

'Dan Tiger'

A green-and-red stripe, this is another variety that was raised by Allan Hawkes.

'Dovey Tiger'

This variety has narrow stripes of brown and gold. Bred by Allan Hawkes.

'Grandby Stripe'

'Grandby Stripe' has a dark purple-maroon body, with white farina stripes.

'Jazz Band'

This variety, orange-brown with narrow gold stripes, has a very irregular outline. 'Jazz Band' is another stripe from Derek Parsons.

'Karen Cordrey'

Formerly known as RN25. This is a very poor stripe, in black and white, that would probably be better classed as a fancy.

'Königin der Nacht'

'Königin der Nacht' (which translates as 'queen of the night') is dark purple with white stripes. This variety was raised by Allan Guest, in 1988, from an 'Error' and 'Singer Stripe' cross.

'Arundell'

'Blackpool Rock'

'Lord Saye en Sele'

'Lord Saye en Sele'

Yellow with light reddish brown stripes and a touch of green. The small flowers are freely produced on this vigorous plant, and it can produce flowers at any time of the year. An easy, undemanding plant that offsets readily.

'Lune Tiger'

This stripe is a red and greeny white – another 'Tiger' raised by Allan Hawkes.

'Macbeth Stripe'

A lovely variety with bold greeny white stripes, dusted in farina, on a rich red ground. Raised by Allan Hawkes and exhibited in 1985.

'Marion Tiger'

Allan Hawkes raised this lovely variety. It is classed as the best of the old type of stripe, because of its smooth, rounded outline. The red ground is striped with meal, and it has a china edge. It was named to honour Jimmy Long, the raiser of 'Virginia Belle' (see photo on page 167 and description on page 168), who lived in the small town of Marion.

'May Tiger'

'May Tiger' has a crimson ground which is delicately striped with lines of farina; these wash off if the plant is watered overhead. It was raised by Allan Hawkes, in 1986, from a 'Rover Stripe' and 'Conservative' cross. Exhibited in 1989.

'Mazetta Stripe'

'Mazetta Stripe' has a maroon-red ground striped in green and white, with an irregular, fretted edge. It was raised by Allan Hawkes.

'Medina Tiger'

Narrow brown stripes on a greenish yellow ground. Bred by Allan Hawkes.

'Merlin Stripe'

Allan Hawkes raised this variety which has light green and red stripes.

'Mersey Tiger'

Another 'Tiger' raised by Allan Hawkes, this one with red stripes.

'May Tiger'

'Mazetta Stripe'

'Rover Stripe'

'Virginia Belle'

'Mrs Davies'

Allan Guest raised this attractive plant from the same parentage as 'Blackpool Rock', and named it after his mother. It has purple and white stripes.

'Ormonde Stripe'

Ox-blood red and white. Bred by Allan Hawkes.

'Orwell Tiger'

Bred by Allan Hawkes, 'Orwell Tiger' has green petals with dark red stripes.

'Papagenu'

A purple-and-white stripe, bred by Allan Guest. It is of poor form but is useful for hybridization.

'Raleigh Stripe'

Crimson, wine or brown on fawn; a striking plant that was bred by Allan Hawkes in 1979 and exhibited in 1983.

'Rover Stripe'

The dark, rich red ground of this variety is striped greyish, greenish yellow. Raised by Allan Hawkes, in 1975, from a striped seedling cross. Shown in 1983. (See photo on page 167.)

'Singer Stripe'

Raised by Allan Hawkes and named after an old bicycle, as are most of his stripes.

'Starsand'

An outstanding blue-and-white stripe from Derek Parsons, with the form and proportion required for a Show auricula.

'Sturmy Stripe'

This is an early Allan Hawkes plant; it has white stripes on a brown ground.

'Tiger Bay'

An attractive stripe raised by Allan Hawkes in 1986. The pips of 'Tiger Bay' are mauve, merging to blue, with fawn stripes.

'Vein'

Lilac ground with green and white striping, from Derek Parsons. This is a striking plant, but lacks the paste centre required for a Show auricula.

'Virginia Belle'

A rich red pip with delicate stripes of meal. Bred by Jimmy Long, in the Blue Ridge Mountains, Virginia, USA. 'Virginia Belle' needs to be grown very carefully as the stripes of farina are easily lost, and it then looks like a self. (See photo on page 167.)

'Whitworth Stripe'

Another plant from Allan Hawkes, 'Whitworth Stripe' has dark stripes.

APPENDIX I

STANDARDS OF THE NATIONAL AURICULA AND PRIMULA SOCIETY

I am very grateful to the National Auricula and Primula Society, Northern Section, for their permission to include the following standards for judging auriculas, including the commentary, which is designed to clarify certain points. These have been printed unedited and in their entirety. I feel they will be of invaluable use to aspiring showmen. The following standards for judging auriculas were adopted at the Committee Meeting of the National Auricula and Primula Society (Northern Section) on 7 February 1998.

GENERAL STANDARDS

The plant as a whole should be compact and well-balanced, with crisp, healthy foliage, preferably a single rosette of leaves of sufficient size to nicely cover the pot. The stem should be strong, elastic and tall enough to hold the truss well above the leaves, but not overly long (between 10 and 18cm [4–7in]), a neat stake may be employed to support the stem. The footstalks should be sufficiently strong to hold the pips in a firm array and of just such a length as to permit each pip to be displayed unoccluded. All the pips in a truss should be of even size and character, the periphery of each should just meet that of its neighbour to form a compact whole. The required number of fully **expanded** pips per truss is schedule dependent.

Show auriculas

Edged

The pip:

1 Should be round and flat with the outline of a solid disc, the individual petals should be of an even size, smooth, free of notches, of good substance and overlap sufficiently to give the desired circular appearance. The four bands should be of equal 'weight', no one dominating or receding. Size is of secondary importance, but pips should be neither too large nor small, 32mm [1¼in] being median.

2 (a) The tube should not exceed one-fourth the diameter of the pip, [should] be round, smooth-edged, golden or rich yellow in colour, of a waxy substance and well up to the plane of the pip.

(b) The **anthers** should be fresh and bold, of the same colour as and evenly set around the tube. They should curve inwards to meet over and obscure the lower tube.

(c) The pistil should not be visible among or above the anthers or the plant is disqualified.

(d) The paste should be circular with clear-cut edges, the outer edge at half of the pip's diameter; the paste should be brilliant white, smooth, dense and free from blemishes and cracks.

(e) The body, or ground colour should be solid and circular where it meets the paste, its outer edge should extend to three-fourths of the pip's diameter, feathered finely into the edge, but not extending to the pip's periphery. It should be bright, rich and velvety, unshaded and free from meal.

(f) The edge may be green, grey or white according to class. If green-edged it should be of an even shade, bright and free of meal. Grey-edged flowers should have an even covering of meal overlying the petal, not so thick as to mask completely the underlying green thereby creating the grey effect. In white-edged flowers the covering of meal should completely mask the green of the petal. In both grey and white edges the meal should be white, bright, refined and free from blemishes.

Selfs

The pips should be somewhat smaller than the edged types, 29mm [1⅛in] being median, but should have the same general character; the petals should be of an even colour, unshaded, bright, clear and smooth, of a velvety texture, free from veins, meal and blemishes. The tube should be smaller than in the edged type, about one-sixth of the pip's diameter, and be well-filled with anthers; pin-eyed plants are disqualified, paste as in 2 (d) above, save that it should extend to just under half the pip's diameter.

STRIPED AURICULAS

General standards as for Show auriculas. The stripes may be of meal and/or colour. The striping should be radial, clearly defined and evenly spread, the stripes should not coalesce to form a body colour as in the edged forms.

ALPINE AURICULAS

General standards as for Show auriculas save that a minimum of five fully expanded pips is required in all open classes. The individual pips should be about the same size as the self's, ie 29mm [1⅛in] being median.

(a) Alpine auriculas may be gold- or light-centred. Depending on type the central disc (eye) should be a bright golden yellow, white or pale cream. The pips should be bright, the petals of a rich velvety texture. The florets should be free from farina.

(b) The tube should be round, about one-sixth the diameter of the pip, well up to the surface of the pip, of the same colour as the eye and well filled with anthers.

(c) Anthers. As in 2 (b) above save that the anthers should be of a rich gold or yellow.

(d) Pistil. As in 2 (c) above.

(e) The eye, abutting the tube, should be a uniform shade, smooth, bright and free from blemishes. The outer edge should be circular, sharply defined and extend to just over half of the pip's diameter.

(f) The individual petals should be of a similar size, un-notched, and shaded evenly from a deeper hue where it joins the eye to a lighter tint at the periphery.

FANCIES

General standards as above save that the flowers do not fulfil the criteria for any of the sections.

DOUBLE AURICULAS

General standards as for Show auriculas. Doubled forms of any type of auricula are acceptable, the doubling may be of any character. A minimum of five fully open pips is required in all classes.

1 The pip should be circular in outline and have at least two full rows of petals plus sufficient additional central petals to completely cover and obscure the tube. The petals should be smooth-edged without notches, their conformation should be neat and regular and effectively fill the pip. Entries with open-centred pips are disqualified. The pips should be of the same size as the Show selfs and Alpines, 29mm [1⅛in] being median.

2 The colour is of secondary importance to form, it may be variegated, shaded, or self-coloured, but should be clear and bright.

3 Where meal is present it must not be 'smeared', but crisp and bright.

COMMENTARY

The foregoing set of standards is based upon those already in use at northern shows with alterations thought necessary to maintain, or improve standards. These notes are intended to supplement the rules, clarify some of the points and serve as an indicator of ideals.

Over the past few years the size of some auriculas on the show bench have grown to the point that they are now presented grossly out of character. One of the aims of the revised rules is to eliminate such, hence the suggested sizes for the florets of the various classes of flowers and acceptable length for the stem. Over-large, or too-small pips, gross foliage, elongated, or too-short stems and weak, or straggly **pedicels** should be penalized when considering the award of prizes.

Traditionally pip sizes have been related to the size of old coins, the florin, half-crown and crown, 32mm (1¼in) recommended for edged pips corresponds to the half crown, 29mm (1⅛in) recommended for self, Alpines and Doubles to the florin.

1 'The tube should be well up to the plane of the pip', ie there should be a crisp division between the plane of the floret and the tube with no falling off of the surface of the pip into the tube.

   Body colours other than black are not excluded from any of the classes for edged auriculas, but the same criteria for judging black ground-coloured plants should be observed, ie they should be bright, unshaded, of the correct proportion and free of meal. No lowering of standards should be entertained to accommodate other ground colours; nondescript colours, dull purples and the like, are not encouraged, but scarlets, blues and such are to be welcomed.

   At the present time striped auriculas do not have the same form as other show auriculas and some latitude is required in interpreting standards within their classes.

2 In the edged classes each of the four bands is of equal importance. The paste should be a smooth band free from extensions of petal edges, so-called cracks. The feathering of the body colour into the petal's edge should be fine and, within reason, encompassed in a regular circle. The outline of the pip should be circular with minimal excursions from the solid outline where the petals meet.

3 Multi-plant classes should stand together harmoniously with no glaring difference in the size of truss or height of plant. Some difference in the height of individual stems is often inevitable in which case the plants should be arranged to their best advantage, usually with the tallest at the rear of the bench graduating to the shortest at the front. The use of outside aids in the staging of plants, ie blocks, or multiple pots, is not permissible.

A multi-plant group should be representative of its section. In the Show section an ideal group should have no preponderance of any one class. In the sixes, not more than two selfs (and those of different classes) should be included. In the fours not more than one self. Multi-plant self classes should contain a variety of colours. Alpine and Double multi-plant classes should be well balanced between the different shades of colours available in the section.

4 Alpines should be gold- or pale-centred. Narrowing of the difference between the two, ie the so-called custard-centres, is not desirable.

   One of the main criteria of the Alpine section is the gradual shading of the colour of the petals from a darker inner hue to a paler tint at the edge. Too abrupt or deficient shading are faults.

5 'Doubled forms of any type of auricula are acceptable', ie no one type, doubled Alpine, self, edged, or Border has preference. 'Doubling may be of any character', ie no particular petal formation or degree of doubling is preferred to another. The criteria is the extent to which the pips on a plant meet the required standards. For show purposes the classifications 'formal' or 'informal' have no relevance.

   An 'open-centred' pip is one in which the central tube is not covered and obscured by petals, so giving the effect of a hole in the centre of the flower. 'Variegated' includes any combination of colours, striping, flecking, etc.

6 Fancies are auriculas that do not fit into any of the accepted classes.

7 Pots may be clay or plastic, but should be round, terracotta in colour and clean.

It is emphasized that, with the exception of the rules concerning pin-eyed flowers and open-centred double pips which require disqualification, the above points are guides to interpreting the show standards and inevitably require discretion on the part of the judges when balancing the differing degrees to which entries meet the laid down standards.

APPENDIX II

TABLE OF AURICULA TROPHIES AND AWARDS

The awards described below are those referred to in 'Introducing the Plants'.
The various auricula societies have similar ranges of trophies and awards.

Award of Merit

Awarded to a winning seedling if it is considered to be exceptional. Quite rare.

Bamford Trophy

This is, I believe, a traditional copper kettle. Donated by Dan Bamford, an eminent Northern (north of England) grower of the 1930s–1950s, to the American Primrose Society for award in the auricula classes at their shows.

Best in Show

Awarded to best plant overall, from all sections.

Corsar Cup

Donated by an old Northern member, Kenneth Corsar, and awarded for the best show seedling. Sadly, the cup was destroyed in a fire and has now been replaced by the Society's Seedling Cup (Northern Section).

Faulkner Trophy

This trophy commemorates the Alpine raiser Frank Faulkner. It is awarded for best exhibitor-raised Alpine.

Premier Awards

These are usually medals. They are awarded to the outstanding plant in each section of the show schedule.

Seedling Cup

The Society's Seedling Cup replaced the Corsar Cup, which was destroyed in a fire. It is awarded to the best show seedling.

GLOSSARY

anther the part of the stamen which bears the pollen

body colour exclusive to the edge and fancy varieties of Show auriculas. The inner margin of the body colour should be smooth and circular, and the outer margin should feather out into the edge

bred this term covers the whole process from hybridization (crossing two selected parent plants), harvesting and germinating seed, raising seedlings to flowering, introducing the plant to the show bench, and naming the variety

calyx the sepals of the flower collectively; the outside part of the unopened flower bud. In auriculas it is usually green

carrot the thick, underground part of the stem, usually near vertical, from which the roots grow

contact this term refers to insecticides which kill predators (eg aphids) through direct contact with their body

corolla the petals of the flower collectively; in auriculas there are 6–9

edge the outer part of an auricula petal which, at some stage, mutated to take on the characteristics and colour of a leaf

expanded the term used to describe a fully open flower

farina (*see* meal)

F1/F2 the first filial generation from a cross is called F1 in botanical shorthand. The progeny of a cross between two F1 seedlings is known as the F2 generation, and so on

flowers of sulphur minute crystals of sulphur, used by gardeners as a fungicide

footstalk known botanically as the pedicel, the stalk of a single flower in a truss

The white edges of 'James Arnot' are the result of a thick dusting of farina

hybridizer a person who deliberately crosses different plant varieties in an attempt to produce new varieties (*see also* raiser)

introduced this refers to when, or by whom, a seedling was first shown or distributed

line breeding continued breeding from related seedlings, crossing and recrossing the progeny of two parents to bring together desirable recessive characteristics; a downside can be the combining of bad or undesirable characteristics

meal also called 'farina', this is the powdery coating that can be present on the leaves, flowers and stems of auriculas

mutation a change in the cell characteristics of a plant, giving rise to a new variety (*see also* sport)

offset an offset is a plantlet thrown out from the roots or stem of an auricula. It can be detached from the parent plant easily and grown on to replicate its parent. A plant is said to offset when it produces such a plantlet

paste the circular ring, which is heavily coated in meal, around the centre of the flowers of Show auriculas. It is usually white and often has a glistening enamel appearance

pedicel (*see* footstalk)

pin-eyed a flower is said to be pin-eyed when the stigma or pin is carried above the stamens. Note that pin-eyed auriculas will be disqualified at the shows – all the named Show and Alpine auriculas are thrum-eyed – but they can be of use in breeding

pip an individual flower. An expanded pip is a fully open flower, and should be flat or nearly flat

pollen fine, powdery grains on the stamens (the male part of the flower). The pollen needs to be transferred to the stigma (the female part of the flower) for fertilization to occur

raiser a person who grows a plant from seed to flowering. Often the hybridizer and raiser of a particular variety will be the same person, but a hybridizer may distribute seed to other growers who then become the raiser of a plant

raised usually synonymous with 'bred' (*see above*), this term is sometimes qualified to indicate that the seed or unflowered seedling came from another grower

reflexed this term describes the backwards bending of the petals below the flat plane of the pip – a fault for show purposes

scape the whole flower stem

sport a mutation whereby a change in the genetic make-up of a plant is passed on to future generations

stamen the male reproductive organ – this bears the pollen

stigma the female reproductive organ, also known as the pin. It is ready to receive pollen when it becomes sticky

systemic this term refers to insecticides that are absorbed into the plant, thus making the plant poisonous to the predator (eg aphids)

thrum-eyed a flower is said to be thrum-eyed when the stamens are above the pin

truss also called an 'umbel', this is one head of flowers

tube this is the part of the flower that contains the stamens, ovary and stigma. It should reach to the flat part of the open flower, be yellow and, viewed from above, circular

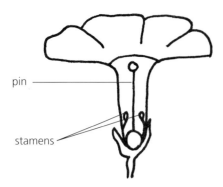

Cross section of a pin-eyed flower

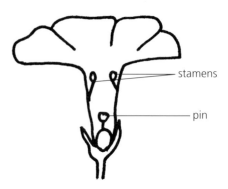

Cross section of a thrum-eyed flower

USEFUL ADDRESSES

NURSERIES SELLING AURICULAS

In addition to the nurseries listed below, there are many specialist alpine and herbaceous nurseries who stock a selection of named auriculas. Any grower with access can find information about nurseries on the Internet.

FRANCE
Monique and Thierry
Dronet
'Un Jardin de Cottage'
Berchigranges
88640 Granges sur Vologne
Tel: 03 29 51 47 19

NETHERLANDS
Elconore de Köning
Kruipuitsedijk 3
4436 RC Oudelande
Netherlands
Tel: 01135-44006

NORWAY
Rolf Eide
Eides Stauder
Kyrkjelemyra 20
5300 Kleppest
Tel: 56 14 18 50

UNITED KINGDOM
Arcadia Nurseries
Brass Castle Lane
Nunthorpe
Middlesbrough

Cleveland TS8 9EB
Tel: 01642 310782
Fax: 01642 300817
E-mail:
janetqueen@arcadian-archives.com
www.arcadian-archives.com
/arcadianurs.htm

Craven's Nursery
1 Foulds Terrace,
Bingley
West Yorkshire BD16 4LZ
Tel: 01274 561412

Farmyard Nurseries
Llandysul
Carmarthenshire
Wales SA44 4RL
Tel: 01559 363389
E-mail: Richard@
farmyardnurseries.co.uk
www.btinternet.com/~farm
yard.nurseries/index.htm

Field House Alpines
Leake Road
Gotham
Nottingham NG11 0JN
Tel: 0115 9830278

Martin Nest Nurseries
Grange Cottage
Hemswell
Gainsborough
DN21 5UP
Tel: 01427 668369
www.martin-nest.
demon.co.uk

W and S Lockyer
39 Mitchley Avenue
Riddlesdown
Purley
Surrey
CR8 1BZ
Tel: 0181 6601336

UNITED STATES
Alston's Primrose Auricula
(Primrose) Nursery
5527 West Branch Trail
Racine WI 53402-1945
Tel: 414 681 2740
E-mail:
auriculas@otcm.com
www.otcm.com/auricula
/photos.htm

AURICULA SOCIETIES

Details on auricula societies, including dates and places of meetings, can be found on the Internet.

UNITED KINGDOM

National Auricula and Primula Society
http://freespace.virgin.net/peter_gavin.ward.ward/index.htm

There is no overall parent body providing centralized functions. The three sections listed below are independent of each other, and self-governing, with their own constitutions, rules and officers.

Northern Section
D. G. Hadfield
146 Queens Road
Cheadle
Cheshire SK8 5HY
Tel: 0161 4856371

Midland and West Section
P. G. Ward
6 Lawson Close
Saltford
Bristol BS31 3LB
Tel: 01225 872893

Southern Section
L. E. Wigley
67 Warnham Court Road
Carshalton
Surrey SM5 3ND
For information please write

UNITED STATES

The American Primrose Society
Treasurer
Fred Graff
2630 W Viewmont Way W
Seattle WA 98199
www.eskimo.net/~mcalpin.htm

Local Chapters
Alaska
Alaska Group
Ed Buyarski
PO Box 33077
Juneau AK 99803-3077
Tel: 907 789 2299
E-mail:
buyarski@alaska.net

Washington
Eastside Chapter
Thea Oakley
3304 288th Ave NE
Redmond WA 98053
Tel: 453 8806177
E-mail: othea@halcyon.com

Tacoma Chapter
Candy Strickland
6911 104th St E
Puyallup WA 98373
Tel: 253 841 4192

Washington Chapter
Rosetta Jones
170 E Dunoon Pl
Shelton WA 98584
Tel: 360 426 7913

Seattle Chapter
June Skidmore
6730 West Mercer Way
Mercer Island WA 98040
Tel: 206 232 5766
E-mail:
JSkidm4011@aol.com

East Coast
Doretta Klaber Chapter
Dot Plyler
18 Bridle Path
Chadds Ford PA 19317
Tel: 610 459 3969

CANADA
British Columbia
British Columbia Primrose Group
Dennis Oakley
10060 Dennis Pl
Richmond BC V7A 3G8
Tel: 604 274 0551

INDEX

ABOUT THE AUTHOR

Over the years, Mary's interest in auriculas developed into a passion and full-time occupation, reputation for her enthusiasm spread, and she became a noted alpine expert and grower.

Mary and Michael Robinson grew auriculas at Martin Nest Nurseries for over 20 years, initially in the Pennines near Huddersfield and then, from 1986, at Hemswell, near Gainsborough, in Lincolnshire (both in the UK).

They won many awards, including several gold medals from the Harrogate Spring Show. In 1996 their auricula collection was awarded National Collection Status.

This is Mary's second book, following *Primulas: The Complete Guide*, first published in 1990. Sadly, she died in 1999, before the publication of this title.